Librarians of Babel

CHANDOS
INFORMATION PROFESSIONAL SERIES

Series Editor: Ruth Rikowski
(email: Rikowskigr@aol.com)

Chandos' new series of books are aimed at the busy information professional. They have been specially commissioned to provide the reader with an authoritative view of current thinking. They are designed to provide easy-to-read and (most importantly) practical coverage of topics that are of interest to librarians and other information professionals. If you would like a full listing of current and forthcoming titles, please visit our web site www.chandospublishing.com or email info@chandospublishing.com or telephone +44 (0) 1223 891358.

New authors: we are always pleased to receive ideas for new titles; if you would like to write a book for Chandos, please contact Dr Glyn Jones on email gjones@chandospublishing.com or telephone number +44 (0) 1993 848726.

Bulk orders: some organisations buy a number of copies of our books. If you are interested in doing this, we would be pleased to discuss a discount. Please info@chandospublishing.com or telephone +44 (0) 1223 891358.

Librarians of Babel

A toolkit for effective communication

PAOLA DE CASTRO

Chandos Publishing

Oxford · Cambridge · New Delhi

b 32253114

Chandos Publishing
TBAC Business Centre
Avenue 4
Station Lane
Witney
Oxford OX28 4BN
UK
Tel: +44 (0) 1993 848726
Email: info@chandospublishing.com
www.chandospublishing.com

Chandos Publishing is an imprint of Woodhead Publishing Limited

Woodhead Publishing Limited
Abington Hall
Granta Park
Great Abington
Cambridge CB21 6AH
UK
www.woodheadpublishing.com

First published in 2009

ISBN:
978 1 84334 378 3

Z
678
.D4
2009

Typeset by Domex e-Data Pvt. Ltd.
Printed in the UK and USA.

Contents

Acknowledgements

The author is grateful to Roberto Aguerre and Marco Pietrangeli for supporting the project of writing this book and to Luisa Marquardt of the University 'Roma 3', Faculty of Education, Rome and Vittorio Ponzani and Renata Solimini of the Istituto Superiore di Sanità for their precious advice in reviewing the manuscript.

Preface

A librarian's main task is to collect, organize and retrieve information and there are many books dealing with these tasks and the challenges coming from the use of information and communication technologies. This book is an introduction to other different and difficult tasks that librarians and information specialists are now called upon to carry out their everyday tasks to guarantee effective communication, among peers, library users, and the general public, through different media. The main elements of professional writing, conference or workshop organization, and PowerPoint presentations will be outlined to help develop professional writing and communication skills even without background information.

The book is concise and easy to understand and can be used for practical purposes. The approach is based on everyday practice rather than on theories.

List of figures

Figures

About the author

Paola De Castro is the head of the Publishing Unit of the Istituto Superiore di Sanita (http://www.iss.it/, the National Institute of Health in Italy) and member of editorial committees of publications edited by the Institute (*Annali dell'Istituto Superiore di Sanita*, a quarterly peer-reviewed science journal), *Notiziario dell'Istituto Superiore di Sanita* (a monthly newsletter on current research and other activities), different series of technical reports and of the journals *European Science Editing* and *Eurosurveillance*. She has published many articles on the information transfer process and research evaluation; delivers courses on scientific writing for Italian National Health Service operators and for the Master in Scientific Communication of the University of Naples. She organizes exhibitions on public health issues addressed to both specialized staff and to the general public, including students. She is involved in a number of activities for the promotion of science culture in schools and also carries out projects on the preservation of historical heritage belonging to scientific institutions (including scientific instruments no longer used for research purposes, unpublished documents, pictures, oral memories). She strongly supports the Open Access model of scientific publishing and is the coordinator of a Coordination and Support Action within the 7FP of the European Union aimed at strengthening collaborations between Europe and Latin America to support scientific writing and Open Access publishing.

A list of publications is available from: http:///www.iss.it/ site/attivita/ISSWEB_istituto/RicercaPersonale/dettaglio.asp ?idAna=1070&lang=1/.

The author may be contacted via the Publishing Unit–Istituto Superiore di Sanità, Rome, Italy.

Website: http://www.iss.it/; e-mail: paola.decastro@iss.it

Introduction

This book is addressed at librarians and information specialists but will not deal with the more traditional tasks usually related with this profession.

We know that librarians work with books and journals, and that they organize information therein contained in order to make it available to all possible users to answer their specific information needs. We also know that this noble activity dates back a very long way; there are traces of the existence of libraries in 3000 BC and there is much historical material testifying their evolution through the centuries.

Today, the main challenge for a librarian is to cope with the ever-increasing amount of information available through different channels, to select and organize it through specific procedures associated with document acquisition, cataloguing, abstracting, indexing, retrieval, storage, preservation, etc. These are the primary activities usually related with the work in a library but they do no longer fit the general idea of librarians as silent people working in silent places, unwilling to speak, and whispering advice in a low voice so as not to disturb scholars' reading. Librarians today dramatically need to communicate even if their profile has long been associated with mystery and obscurity: monks in ancient monasteries frequently were the only keepers of the secrets of the 'Houses of tablets' or the 'Houses of books', as the Sumerians or ancient Egyptians used to call the library. For centuries, they have often been the only ones able to preserve and disclose precious hidden truths: to unveil the history of world 'disasters', the mysteries of human creativity, behaviours, and discoveries.

Their primary role was to accumulate knowledge to build up the 'Book of Humanity' containing all books ever written in the world. They might also become obsessed with the idea of a universal knowledge, as Jorge Luis Borges clearly states in *The Library of Babel* where the library becomes the universe itself, composed of every possible book that can exit through the permutation of all letters within a set number of pages, thus coming to be the universe: a geometrical creature open to any paradox of infinity. (J.L. Borges, the famous writer, was also the Director of the National Library of Argentina.)

This book is intended to give useful suggestions to the 'Librarians of Babel', to facilitate communication and overcome the confusion that sometimes prevents the development of a useful exchange of ideas.

The librarians' role has developed throughout the centuries, as well as the physical support of information passing from votive stelai to gravestones, from papyrus to paper manuscripts, from printed books to digital and multimedia material. Libraries are now changing and dynamic places, and librarians' responsibility far exceeds that of information keepers. There is no doubt that the information and communication technologies have completely upset the library scenario with a dramatic impact on librarians' work and a complete revolution of the most consolidated rules and procedures that have been governing library activities for many centuries.

As the President of the American Library Association (ALA), Leslie Burger, stated, 'Libraries are continuously reinventing themselves in an effort to provide a multitude of programs and services for their users. In many communities the local library serves as a cultural centre, technology training centre, cyber café, or community centre'. (Lecture delivered at the American University of Rome, on 27 April 2007).

The above is briefly why librarians today dramatically need to communicate: to spread information literacy that directly impacts on organizations, systems, and individuals. Libraries are thus becoming a meeting place to find and acquire information, participate in workshops or conferences on different subjects, talk with experts in specific fields, learn, meet friends, and so on. All this requires that librarians become aware of the necessity to participate in continuous education programmes and share ideas at different levels in the awareness of the new opportunities created by the information and communication technologies.

In other fields of science, writing or speaking skills are already included in academic curricula and are recognized as valuable performance and evaluation parameters. Just think of the career of researchers who struggle with the 'publish or perish syndrome' obliging them to publish in high-impact journals to receive funds for research and professional advancement. Communication, in its different facets, oral and written, is becoming also fundamental for librarians of the third millennium.

Based on personal experience in teaching scientific writing to medical staff, and in organizing conferences, workshops, and exhibitions, this book is addressed to young librarians having basic knowledge of library activities but who might lack experience in tackling all the other tasks related to communication, such as writing an article or a technical report, organizing a conference or a workshop, or preparing a PowerPoint presentation.

This book may also be useful to older colleagues who may not be familiar with the techniques and strategies concerning such activities that are carried out in a library in parallel with the most traditional ones. Suggestions given are based on experience rather than on theories; they should be considered as a first step towards a multitasking profession that needs continuous updating, flexibility, creativity, and much commitment and devotion.

I have spent over 20 years working in a publishing unit of a governmental research institute, the 'Istituto Superiore di Sanità', the National Health Institute of Italy, that deals with research for public health (http://www.iss.it). When I began my career, PCs were not much used yet and, of course, neither the Internet. So, many things dramatically changed in a rather short span of time, and I am an eye witness of a Copernican revolution in the information chain. I have always been in close contact with the library and documentation services of my institute and have had the opportunity to closely perceive the difficulties that library staff may encounter in writing an article or a technical report, producing a conference poster or presentation.

Communication is becoming more and more a fundamental part of our daily activities.

That is why librarians should be able to recognize which is the right way to express their ideas and overcome the anxiety and frustrations coming from the vicious circle of inadequateness appearing in *The Library of Babel* where nobody is able to understand the real sense of things.

As information professionals, librarians today take part in conferences, deliver papers, write articles, reports, pamphlets, participate in the creation of institutional repositories, contribute to the creation and development of library websites, teach users how to retrieve information, how to use and exploit Internet resources, take part in e-learning projects, etc.

As members of a growing community, they also produce their own journals that may be issued by professional associations, libraries in research institutes, universities, schools, or by commercial publishers. Some of these journals also have 'impact factor', which is a highly recognized attribution indicating how many times, on average, papers appearing in a journal are cited in a given period of time. This means that they have been selected and recognized as quality journals on the basis of a measure.

Impact factor is generally considered a quality measure even if it is based on a quantitative account of citations received by journals articles in a 2-year period. The assignment of impact factor is a rather controversial issue, nevertheless it has a dramatic influence in journal quality assessment all over the world. It is interesting to know that Eugene Garfield, the founder of the Institute of Scientific Information-today Thompson Corporation assigning the impact factor to selected journals-was a librarian; he first mentioned the idea of an impact factor in 1955, without any minimal idea of its future developments.

All this considered, there is no doubt that librarians must acquire the most appropriate skills for effective communication not only among peers, but also towards library users, students, the media, etc. An effective communication guarantees a proper professional development and career advancement.

Many initiatives are now being developed at national and international levels to improve professional communication. The editorial quality of library and information science publications, for example, is a relevant performance indicator, and editorial training is often included in the education programmes of LIS professionals: among others, the European Association of Health Information and Libraries (EAHIL, http://www.eahil.net/) is also promoting training courses in editorial matters as an example to be followed by other national and international associations. This new form of collaboration between librarians and editors is very useful to produce better information tools and improve communication at all levels.

This book wishes to contribute to empower librarians with proper tools to tackle communication challenges; it does not have the pretence of being exhaustive (oral communication is not specifically treated), but to provide ideas and strategies that can be helpful in everyday activities. It develops from a general idea of communication, focuses on the importance of the aims and targets of any message and gives hints and tips on how to develop correct written communication and produce documents that will fit best the selected channel (journal articles, books, conference papers, posters, etc.). Elements that are common to each channel, such as using illustrations or writing references are presented separately. The reading of the different chapters may follow a personal path that is not necessarily the one presented in the book.

The communication process

Librarians of the third millennium need to communicate and they should be aware of the different opportunities and strategies they have to properly deliver any message. We should consider the basic rules that stand behind any communication process that forms an essential part of the toolkit of the 'Librarian of Babel'. This will allow useful reflections that contribute to the most correct and effective transmission of a message that is so crucial both at work and in personal life. So often, in fact, many initiatives fail or do not reach the desired objective, just because of communication barriers.

Key elements

In the broadest sense, communication can be intended as every exchange of information (of any kind) between individuals that involves at least one sender and one receiver. Communication skills, including both oral and written communication, can be improved by becoming aware of the basic elements involved in the process and the specific roles of each one of them.

The process is clearly shown in Figure 1.1 where you can see how it develops from sender to receiver, thanks to a common code and an appropriate transmission channel. The essential elements of the communication process are outlined to give a general idea of the dynamics of communication; the

Figure 1.1   Elements of the communication process

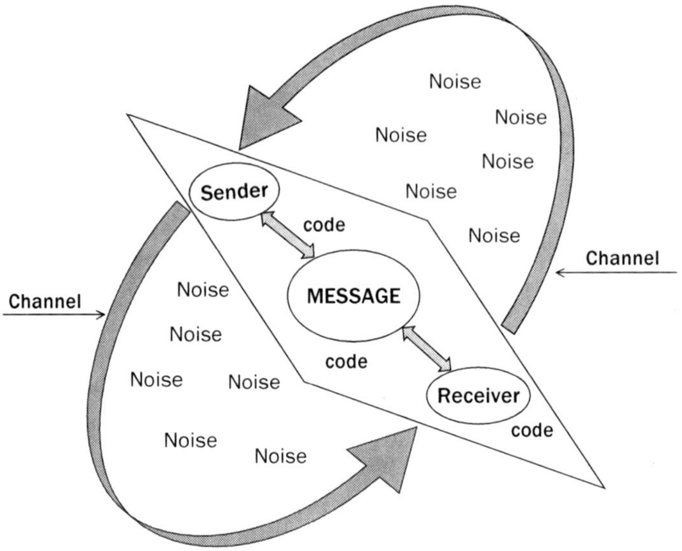

process is only apparently simple. The figure does not include the initial input behind the communication process: the necessity, wish, duty or responsibility to share something (an idea, a feeling, a service, etc.) with someone else, which is the prerequisite of the entire process.

Sender

The sender (or encoder) is someone who starts the communication process to accomplish something. He/she is moved by an idea, an objective, a need, a feeling, etc., for example, 'I wish to write an article to communicate a research project, share an experience, look for collaborations, etc. Or, I wish to take part in a conference, or I need to receive/give information on a specific topic, etc.'.

The sender may be not conscious of his/her motivation when communicating in an informal way; however, in any formal communication such initial input should be very carefully evaluated because it directly influences any following step. The sender (a speaker in a conference, an author of a book, a group leader, etc.) will develop a message, as explained below, and encode it—using words or images— to transmit it to the receiver. Both formal and informal communication have their own rules and procedures (e.g. instructions to authors of a journal article, time schedules in a conference, unwritten traditions or other codes in different kinds of communication, etc.).

Message

The message is the objective of communication: it is intended to inform, teach, convince, give or receive credit, visibility, etc. Formal communication, different from other types of relationships among individuals, should have clear and well defined objectives. The message, which may take different shapes, is encoded by the sender, who uses a channel to transmit it to the receiver. In the following chapters of this book, you will see how the same message (idea) can be properly adjusted to fit both to the target (receiver) and the channel in order to guarantee an effective communication.

In this book, we should essentially deal with verbal communication that is expressed through oral or written words, and reflect upon the different possible choices that a librarian can have to spread an idea. Any choice must take into account any existing rules and traditions.

We should consider, however, that also non-verbal communication (conscious and/or unconscious actions and behaviours) has a fundamental role in *vis a vis* communication process, be it formal or informal. It is generally defined as the body language, including gestures, postures, eye contact, facial expressions, appearance, active listening, etc. Also all kinds of images including photographs, films, maps, tables, graphs, videos are part of non-verbal communication and represent key elements in both written papers or oral presentations (see Chapter 7).

Code

In this framework, a code is a shared way of representing the same meaning. It is a system of rules used by a group to communicate. Encoding is the process by which information—that is meaning—is converted into another form of representation (code).

In the communication process, the sender encodes the message. Decoding is the reverse process that allows converting back the code into information that is understandable by the receiver. The receiver, in turn, can decode the message only when he is able to manage the same code; therefore, senders and receivers must share at least a minimum set of the same code in order to make communication possible. Language is a perfect example of a common code that allows communication among groups of individuals.

Channel

It is the physical medium by which communication is transmitted; it is the path through which information passes from sender to receiver and backwards. It may be oral, print, digital or other, and it should be carefully evaluated before operating a selection (particularly in formal communication), reflecting on the receiver's capabilities to decode the meaning of the message, and its objectives. In some cases a written channel (paper, web page, leaflet, etc.) may be more appropriate to transmit a message; in others, oral communication may be more effective also considering that *vis a vis* communication allows a precious immediate feedback from receiver.

Receiver

The receiver is the person or group whom the communication is addressed to. As decoder of the message, the receiver should share the same code of the sender in order to understand the message and interpret its meaning. The receiver does not have a passive role in the communication process as he/she transmits feedback to the receiver and may activate a circular process becoming himself a sender of a message.

Noise

Noise is anything that interferes with the communication and, therefore, disturbs or prevents the correct transmission of the message from sender to receiver. Noise is not only, or not just, physical, such as any secondary signal that obscures or obliterates some portion of the main signal. Noise today is mainly intended as a metaphor indicating all those elements (actions, facts, physical elements, etc.) that may interfere in the correct transmission of the message.

Feedback

It is the action coming back to the sender after receivers have decoded the message. It is a key component of the process because it allows the sender to evaluate the effectiveness of his message. It is the final, fundamental link in the chain and is represented by the recipient's response or reaction of the receiver to the message. It may have different forms according to the contest where the communication process takes place.

It may be a spoken comment, a sigh, a smile, a long silence, a written message, a citation in a paper, a changing attitude, or any other action. A lack of response is also a form of response. Without feedback, the sender cannot confirm that the receiver has interpreted the message correctly. Feedback is fundamental both in oral and written communication and provides an opportunity for the sender to take the necessary corrective actions when he realizes that the message is not completely understood or misunderstood. It plays a fundamental role in communication and determines the success of the entire process. There are different kinds of feedback that may be immediate or not, expressed or silent and may also help to detect those barriers that reduce or prevent a successful communication such as differences in background, different interpretations of words or understanding of the language, and differing emotional reactions.

From theories to practice

A theoretical background is necessary to better reflect on the different implications behind any communication choice, but experience often teaches much more than theories.

The first important element to start any formal communication is the analysis of the message that you wish to transmit, the target (receiver) whom such message is addressed to and the results expected from its transmission.

The choice is apparently easy; indeed it requires careful evaluation of different factors that will contribute to the success of the initiative. The rule of the five 'W' (who, what, why, where, when), traditionally used to teach on how to report information for newspaper articles, may represent a good starting point. In fact, it may be useful to ask yourselves *who* is the target of the message (community of peers, general public, adults, children, etc.); *what* kind of message is it (prescription, advice, research activity, etc.); *why* it is important to spread it; *where* is the story set (study, event, research, etc.); *when* in time did or will it be delivered.

And we may add more questions:

- Is the content appropriate for the target or intended audience?

- Is the message original? Or are there other similar stories (studies, research, recommendations, etc.)? Did I check the bibliography on that subject? Does my idea add something to the existing knowledge? Will it be applicable in a larger framework?

- Does the intended target really need this information? Will they be able to get its meaning, will they be aware of its importance, or should I convince them that it will be useful?

- Is the message coherent with my institute's objective? Will it be appreciated and supported by my supervisors?

If you are able to give an answer to most of the above questions and the 'I don't know', 'I am not really sure' answers are just a few, then you should reflect on the most appropriate *channel* to spread your message and ask yourselves:

- Which is the best way to transmit my idea? (oral, written, digital, all of these, others?)

- In the case of oral communication, where should my message be delivered? In a meeting, a conference, a workshop, a lesson, or others?

- In the case of written communication, will it be published as a journal article, a book, a technical report, a leaflet, a poster, or others?

- When will the presentation take place or the manuscript be published? (Do I have enough time to prepare it properly, and is there a set deadline or may I postpone or anticipate it?)

- Who will collaborate with me on this work? Colleagues from my own institution or others institutions, experts in the field, or should I do the work alone? Last, but not least,

- What is the budget? Is it possible to rely on external collaborations? Can I, or my institution, afford to pay page charges, or any other editorial or printing expenses in the case of written communication? or travel and accommodation expenses, or registration fees in the case of a conference presentation?

All these questions need to be clarified before deciding which is the best path to walk on. Good sense and opportunity considerations very often represent the basic ingredients for the best choice; then enthusiasm and determination always contribute very strongly to guarantee the final achievement.

Finding your own rules

Once you have decided that a piece of information—generally intended as any kind of intellectual production—is worth circulating, you should find the best way to get the message across. Each channel has its own rules, but there is no one formula applicable to any situation in order to communicate successfully.

In each single case, you should be able to find out the most appropriate strategy to define the best 'marketing mix' that will work for that situation by considering all the dynamics in the communication set, including any form of possible noise.

In some cases, rules may be easily available; in others you should ask and look for them. For example, in journal articles or other kinds of written communication, authors are given specific instructions to follow ('Instructions to authors', 'Guide to authors', 'House style manuals', etc.). These represent an important guide for the production of a valuable manuscript, although they are never exhaustive. There are always unexpressed rules or good practices that are more difficult to retrieve or that come from more or less consolidated traditions, unwritten or local conventions, practice.

A general rule is that everything may communicate: from the way a manuscript is submitted for publication to the editor in chief of a journal (a shabby look is generally associated with a poor paper), to a prolonged pause in an oral presentation (that may have many positive or negative meanings), from the position of institutional logos in the layout of the first page of a book, to the size and font of typographical characters, from the reaction or lack of reactions of your colleagues or boss, to the way you are dressed, from the colours of an illustration, to the folders used for conference papers, and so on.

The analysis of the different factors that play a part in the communication set is fundamental to operate a selection. For example, the library of a research institute has different objectives from a school library or a public one and of course librarians need to use different strategies to communicate similar messages to their users. Yet, the same librarians of a research institute or a public library meeting in a conference or writing an article for a professional journal will have to refer to the same rules and procedures, use the same styles for references, respect the same copyright laws.

The following chapters of this book will give you hints on some general tips on how to write a paper, organize a conference, and prepare a PowerPoint presentation. It is worth recalling that technology today helps a lot to perform many activities and save time; however, before using these technologies you must be aware of the philosophy behind any communication process that primarily involves individuals with their own human complexities, and not computers having different kinds of technical complexities! Computers are useful tools but before using them, you must have a clear idea of the results you want to get.

2

What you should know before writing a paper

Writing is not an easy task; it requires good ideas, but also much effort, concentration and time. Therefore, if you decide to write something to be published, be sure that it is worthwhile and useful to somebody else, apart from representing one more item to add to your résumé.

Your work should be original and add something to what has already been published; your editor, publisher and audience should be interested in such a work and you should be able to make your story pleasant, reasonable, and clear; and therefore, cope with all difficulties associated with this commitment.

So, when you decide to write a paper, you should have already identified your key message, your target, and searched the literature to be sure that nothing similar has been written already. Electronic databases now help a lot to make a rapid survey of what has been published, and librarians more than any others have the opportunity to easily search online catalogues and other appropriate sources. Repetitive works are seldom appreciated; furthermore, reviewers usually detect duplicates and readers will make the rest to discredit your reputation.

Before you start writing any paper, it is important to consider the different types of documents that may host your message, each one having its own characteristics associated to physical nature (shape, material, size, volume, ink, colour, etc.) and to intellectual content (subject matter, language, etc.). Such characteristics are directly related to and influence the aim and target of your message and determine the working procedures leading to the realization of the document.

Also, within each publication type there is a very large choice of possible alternatives; for example, if you decide that a journal article is the most appropriate channel for your paper, then you should select the right journal to submit the paper, whether national or international, peer reviewed or not, indexed in specialized databases, having an impact factor, etc. Then carefully check the journal scope, editorial committees, readership, review process, availability, instructions to authors, etc. Even within the same journal there are different kinds of papers.

To cut a very long story short, the author as producer of information has the primary responsibility of identifying the key message, its intended target and the best channel to spread it.

However, this is only the beginning of a complex process that will require many other important choices and much commitment on your behalf, as authors, before involving the other actors of the editorial chain (editors, editorial assistants, copy-editors, illustrators, photographers, etc.) that will play their role in the editorial process and, therefore, adding value to the original document.

Authors should become aware of the different stages that their paper will pass before publication; this will allow them understand why it is so important to properly fulfil the editorial rules and procedures.

Librarians are used to identify the bibliographic characteristics associated to both traditional printed sources and digital documents, and how to process them. Yet they may be surprised to discover the complexities of the editorial world behind the production of such documents and the roles of the different actors in the editorial chain. Consequently, they may find themselves mystified by their double role of organizers and gatekeepers of the information produced by others, and authors of information they themselves may produce.

Furthermore, the transformations introduced by the widespread use of personal computer and desktop publishing have deeply affected most traditional working procedures in both the production and diffusion of documents; such transformations were further pushed forward by the Internet revolution, which created—in a relative short span of time (no more than 20 years)—a completely new model for producing, exploiting and disseminating intellectual output and upsetting some of the most traditional principles that for centuries have been governing the process of transferring information.

Just think, for example, of the responsibilities assigned to authors, editors and publishers by oversimplifying their roles: authors are primarily responsible for the intellectual production; editors tailor such information according to the target and also guarantee its quality; publishers are responsible for the production and marketing of the final product. Indeed the process is not that easy, as there are many specific tasks and responsibilities assigned to each group, and many other professional figures contributing to the quality of the final product. Yet, complexities have been increasing as we are living in a period of transformation where many of the professional figures of the past are being replaced by new ones having different skills and responsibilities: authors are becoming desktop wizards; editors and sometimes even publishers of their own publications; readers that for centuries had been playing a primary but silent role in the editorial chain, are now allowed to take part in the development of existing documents by adding their own comments on publications directly online, and by creating individual reading paths following different hyper-textual links.

The final result of all this is still to be argued. What is sure is that when playing different overlapping roles, we often feel frustrated in the acquisition of new skills that are only apparently easy to perform.

The editorial process

The editorial process involves all those activities related to manuscript handling, which eventually lead to its publication and distribution. The manuscript, in fact, passes on to many desks before reaching its final form. The editorial process gives added value to the manuscript, and it directly depends on the type of publication and on the procedures established for its review that indeed take most of the time and effort on the editorial side. For example, staff are needed to log in and track manuscripts, keep contact with editors and authors, ensure that established editorial policies and related matters are maintained, etc. The handling of manuscripts may be centralized in a single office (including the secretarial staff) or there may be assistant editors working in different fields and also in different places. Today geographical distance is no longer a problem: in fact, communication through the net makes things much easier and faster than in the past.

In some cases, activities may be concentrated in a very small group of persons (even one person alone may play different roles at the same time); in others, there may be a large team at work for one publication or one journal issue. In case of peer reviewed journals, for example, the manuscript 'voyage' from desk to desk may be very long and require much effort and waiting times even when communication is via e-mail.

Document types

As we have already mentioned, the type of document that contains the message to be delivered to our readers directly influences the editorial process.

To better understand the whole process, we should keep the classic distinction between the most common types of written documents as that between *books* and *journals* that now can be available either in print or digital format or both.

Books represent a work produced by one or more authors dealing with a specific subject, *journals*, represent a collection of works written by different authors and grouped together in a single issue, within a series having a regular frequency.

Of course both books and journals represent only a large categorization used to identify some types of documents with similar characteristics; however, inside these two large groups there are many different document types with specific characteristics (handbooks, manuals, novels, encyclopaedias, magazines, scientific, scholarly or academic journals, society journals, newsletters, etc.). Moreover, journals may contain many different kinds of contributions included in specific sections (editorials, articles, reviews, brief notes, viewpoints, report from meetings, etc.)

Then there is a large number of documents generally included under the umbrella term of *grey literature*, i.e. all the material produced by governments, academics, business and industry that is *not* controlled by commercial publishing: reports, thesis, conference proceedings, leaflets, etc.

Until some decades ago, grey literature was very difficult to retrieve as it was produced only in limited number of copies (the Internet could not help then) and it often lacked the basic bibliographic elements allowing its identification. Yet it was, and still is, an important primary source of precious and unique information in many fields.

Furthermore, today, the use of the Internet has created *new types of documents*: these initially represented only the counterpart of the traditional ones appearing in print, then overlapped with them and, more recently, have developed into new kinds of digital material: blogs, wikis, personal internet pages, pre-prints and post prints in digital archives, discussion lists, etc.

Different consideration should be given to the documents prepared for the *press* for usage by the media that follow other specific rules.

We must also consider that electronic publishing is publishing; therefore, in the interests of the entire community, any kind of information published through the Internet should follow the ethical and also technical recommendations applied to paper copies. Quality, clarity and consistency, for example, are a must for any type of publication, as well as ethical considerations or copyright issues that equally apply to paper and electronic documents. On the contrary, the nature of electronic publishing requires special consideration to allow identifying the proper credentials of each source (copyright, site ownership, etc.) and to guarantee their preservation in time. Librarians as keepers of knowledge through centuries should be aware of their responsibilities in the safeguard and preservation of digital documents that may be so evanescent and unstable in the net.

So, before analysing the characteristics of specific types of publications, it is worth reflecting on some general principles that will help librarians—as authors and sometimes editors or publishers of publications—to create and distribute accurate, clear and easily accessible documents.

We should therefore consider some ethical principles related to the process of evaluating, improving, and publishing a manuscript and the relationships between editors, authors, peer reviewers, and the media. Then we should address the more technical aspects of preparing and submitting manuscripts to be published as *journal articles, books, technical reports,* or *conference papers.* The use of illustrations (tables and figures), references and editorial revision are common features to any kind of written publications and they will be dealt with separately.

Ethical considerations

Ethical considerations regard the roles and conduct of authors, editors and contributors of a paper, including reviewers, editorial staff and publishers. They all contribute to guarantee the quality of the editorial product not only as regards its content but also as regards the fair use of the information collected in the respect of the correctness, truth, rightness, appropriateness, copyright, suitability, privacy and confidentiality, etc.

Authors, editors, contributors, owners and publishers

The question of authorship has often been debated, because apart from the assignment of intellectual property and the inclusion in the authors' catalogues—whose relevance is well known to all librarians—it also has other important career, social, and financial implications, especially in the academic world where priority in publication may be an essential attribute to establish rights on research.

The '*author*' of a document (a journal article, a book, a technical report or even a conference presentation or a poster) is someone who has given a relevant intellectual contribution to the work or research reported in the document itself, by taking part in the conception and design of the study, or data acquisition, analysis and interpretation (first condition). At the same time, authorship credit also includes document drafting or critically revising for important intellectual content (second condition), and approval of the final draft (third condition). According to some authoritative sources (take, for example, the so-called 'Vancouver style' for biomedical publications (http://www.icmje.org) one of the above conditions alone should not be sufficient to be considered an author as authors are responsible for the integrity of the work as a whole. In some academic environments, it is not surprising to find 'ghost' authors that are people taking part in the production of a paper, but—for different reasons—not included in the authors' list.

Although most people expect honesty, there may be many circumstances under which honesty criteria are not followed in publication authorship and in-house policies regarding who can and should be listed as an author are often very controversial. Unfortunately, there are also many cases of 'gift' authors representing someone appearing as an author in the by-line but do not properly deserving such an attribution.

Young authors should clarify their authorship rights at the start of a project to avoid disappointment at the end, and senior authors should show humility and accept other forms of acknowledgement when authorship is not really appropriate.

The order of the names of the authors on the by-line may have a different burden according to specific traditions; generally the first author has a primary role, but in any case, the order should be a joint decision of all the co-authors. It is important to include both the first and the family names of all authors to prevent possible confusion with authors with similar initials. In academic papers the name of the authors is followed by the name of the institutions where they worked at the moment the paper is realized (affiliation).

Editors of books, that contain more consolidated information, do not generally have problems in identifying the author or authors of a volume; however, it is not always the case for the authors of a research paper or other scientific publications reporting, for example, a study that has been realized thanks to the contribution of many individuals. In the case of multiple authors, detailed information about the contributions of each person named as author can be given in the text. This practice is sometimes followed in the academia for career-related reasons.

Another case of authorship that needs consideration is that of documents containing *contributions of different authors* (i.e. books with chapters written by different persons or conference proceedings). Such documents may be 'edited by' one or more individual persons—the editors, who are responsible for the book as a whole (the names of the editors will appear on the cover of the document and on the front page; the names of the authors of each chapter or section will appear inside the text).

All the other contributors who collaborated to the realization of a document—who do not meet the criteria for authorship or editorship—should be listed in an acknowledgements section. Examples of those who might be acknowledged include a person who provided purely technical help, writing assistance, or a department chair that provided only general support. Financial and material support should also be acknowledged. The name of translators may also appear in the acknowledgement section or in a more relevant position provided that no confusion is created between the author of the documents and its translator.

Groups of persons who have contributed materially to the paper but whose contributions do not justify authorship may be listed under a different heading such as 'participating investigators,' and their function or contribution should be described—for example, as 'scientific advice', 'critical review of the study proposal', or 'data collection'.

As regards *editors*, in the widest sense of the term, i.e. journal or book editors, are the people who decide which manuscripts deserve to become journal articles or books. They are responsible to readers, and should be aware of their needs and interests and at the same time guarantee a quality publication. The editor of a journal as well as the editor of a book, or conference proceedings, is the person responsible for its entire content; editorial responsibility may be shared among other persons according to the publishing enterprise and the type of publication. In journals, the *Editor in Chief* takes the responsibility of the publication as a whole, but is supported by other editors or editorial advisors as well as the *referees* (in case of peer-reviewed journals)—see next section—who substantially contribute to the final decision on the quality of the papers to be published.

Sometimes the relationship between editors and owners or publishers of a publication may not be immediately clear. The organization may vary according to existing traditions and type of documents; however, in general, the publishers and/or owners, in their role as managers in the information chain, are responsible for the marketing of the editorial products and besides looking for the readers needs, they also take care of the promotion, pricing and distribution of the final product.

The owners and editors of any published work (either books or journals) have a common goal: the publication of reliable and readable material, produced with due respect for the stated aims and consideration for costs. The balance between market profit and quality content is to be carefully considered and in some cases may be a very delicate one. For example, the owners of a journal generally take important business decisions but with regard to the editorial content of the publication they appoint an editor (Editor in Chief) who represents the authority in any decision regarding content. An independent editorial advisory board may be useful in helping the editor to establish and maintain the editorial policy.

In many cases, the owner of a journal, a newsletter, a report series, or other kinds of publications, may be represented by non-commercial institutions having the role of *issuing organizations*. This is the case, for example, of many governmental or professional institutions editing their own publications. In such cases, the institutions are responsible for both the quality and costs of publication and distribution and they should have to guarantee that the documents they issue are reliable and readable, produced with due consideration for the aims and mission of the institution. The institution as editor of publications should establish and maintain a sound editorial policy and may be supported by internal or external advisory boards or other editorial services.

Libraries within an institution may play the part of non-commercial publishers producing and circulating their own publications (newsletters, reports, etc.). In taking such responsibility, librarians as editors of their own publications should become aware of existing editorial rules to produce quality publications that respect the specific regulations in force in each country.

Peer review process

Evaluation of the publication worthiness of manuscripts (books, handbooks, conference proceedings, journal articles, etc.)

is traditionally based on a referee system, whose objective is to uphold the quality and reputation of the editorial products. This value system leading to the selection of papers for publication has been firmly laid down since the initial development of journals produced in academies in the seventeenth century, even if it is now subject to some more or less considerable criticism and intense debates.

The peer review refers to an assessment given by peers, that is by persons belonging to the same community of knowledge, or experts in the same subject matter. The process is represented by a critical, unbiased and independent assessment of scholarly work. It is part of the scientific process aiming to guarantee the publication of high-quality information. Indeed, peer review may be applied to different fields to evaluate professional performance (teaching activities, programme developments, grant proposals, etc.). Generally, the aim of the process is to evaluate the adequacy of a work in relation to the specifications requested and at the same time identify any possible deviations providing suggestions for improvement.

Peer review, which has been at the heart of the scientific process for over 300 years, is now applied to journal articles as a critical assessment of manuscripts carried out by experts who are not part of the editorial staff; a review process, be it peer review or a more informal or technical review, is always highly recommended for any kind of publications.

Reviewers support the editors in the assessment of papers; this process is sometimes criticized due to possible bias that may influence the judgement of the manuscript; however, there is no doubt that it contributes to improving the quality of the publication. Review may be *open*, i.e. when the authors know the names of reviewers and reviewers know the names of authors, or *blinded*, when the authors do not know the names of reviewers; there is also the case of *double-blinded* review when reviewers are not shown the names of the authors. Each case has its own advantages and disadvantages as knowing the names of authors may inevitably influence the judgement of a paper, in a positive or negative way, even unconsciously. On the other hand, authors knowing the names of their referees may be induced not to accept their comments in a positive way and some disputes may arise.

Peer review is a relevant point under discussion for documents that are informally produced and circulate without any quality control, also through the deposit in digital archives, that is when authors themselves may decide to use an alternative way to disseminate information following one of the options proposed by the 'open access' publication model. The open access model supports the free online circulation of information through open access journals and the deposit in digital archives of documents at different stages in the publication process (pre-print, post-print, published paper).

Indeed revision, if not peer review in its strictest sense—is always highly recommended (see Chapter 9 of this book) and authors should become aware of the responsibility behind the dissemination of their documents that may even provoke unexpected damages.

As an example, just think of some scientific documents dealing with security issues or containing sensitive data that might not be used properly by malevolent readers. This is why special attention must be placed before dissemination of any document to make authors aware of the potential risks of spreading hazardous information. A careful editorial revision of the text or other review or peer review procedures will help to check the quality of information and evaluate the opportunity of the circulation of such data. Also readers should immediately grasp the difference between reviewed and not reviewed sources.

Conflicts of interest

The question of conflicts of interest is a delicate issue that may influence the editorial process at different stages. Conflicts of interest exist when an author (or the authors' institution), a reviewer, an editor, or any other member of the editorial staff have financial or personal relationships that inappropriately influence (bias) his or her actions. These relationships may have negligible or great potential to influence judgement. They may be related to dual commitments, competing financial interests, competing loyalties, etc.

Financial relationships are the most easily identifiable conflicts of interest. However, conflicts may occur also for other reasons, such as personal relationships or academic competition.

Many journals ask their authors to sign a declaration regarding any possible conflicts of interest (personal relationships that might bias their work, involvement with the supporting source or sponsors, etc.). The editors may decide whether to publish such disclosure of conflict of interest.

Also reviewers and/or the other members of the staff involved in the editorial process should disclose any conflicts of interest that could bias their activity, and they should not accept to review specific documents if they believe it to be inappropriate.

Copyright

Copyright issues often represent a crucial point for both authors and editors. Authors are not always aware of their rights (rights of authors) and duties (respect of the rights of the other authors) associated with intellectual property. Furthermore, copyright laws are not the same in all countries and publishers' copyright policies are often updated thus creating added confusion to those who are not directly involved in matters related to copyright management.

The literary meaning of copyright (generally indicated with (c) or the symbol ©) is related to the 'the right to copy' an original creation; following the Anglo-Saxon tradition, copyright is indeed a set of rights regarding intellectual property and regulating the use and circulation of ideas in their different expressions. As mentioned, copyright laws may differ according to both the national and international legislation and to the editorial policy followed by the editors and publishers. In most cases, copyright has a limited duration, generally the life of the author plus either 50 or 70 years, according the legislation in force.

Without going deep into the details of the copyright history, which is rather complex, it is worth mentioning that since the end of the nineteenth century international conventions have been developing to harmonize intellectual property rights worldwide. In particular, the Paris Convention of 1883 and the Bern Convention for the Protection of Literary and Artistic Works first signed in 1886, created the initial framework for international integration of different kinds of intellectual property, including creative, intellectual or artistic works in all their different expressions as well as patents, trademarks and industrial designs, etc. In 1996 the World Intellectual Property Organization (WIPO, http://www.wipo.int/) was established as a specialized agency of the United Nations dedicated to developing a balanced and accessible international intellectual property system, which rewards creativity, stimulates innovation and contributes to economic development while safeguarding public interest.

Publishers' copyright policies are now changing very rapidly as a consequence of the new models of publication following the open access paradigm. In the past, journal and book publishers regularly asked authors to transfer over to them the copyright of their works; authors inevitably signed the *copyright transfer agreement* as there were few alternatives to spread information other than via the commercial circuit. Because of this authors lost the right to use the intellectual content of their papers and were obliged to ask permission to the copyright owner whenever they wanted to re-publish them.

Today, thanks to the Internet and new technologies, a new publishing model—sustaining the free circulation of information—is being developed, and authors are acquiring new marketing powers to manage their rights. For these reasons, there is now an ever-increasing number of journals' and books' editors that do not require authors to transfer over to them the copyright in an exclusive way, as had happened in the past. Authors should be aware that it is now possible to negotiate with editors the rights associated with their works (copy, reproduction, distribution, etc.) by signing a 'non-exclusive transfer agreement'. Furthermore, the development of digital archives where authors themselves can deposit their works even before publication (pre-print or post-print) improves the circulation of information; however, at the same time this requires additional skills to manage the new publishing model. A useful reference source on publishers' copyright policies and self-archiving is Sherpa/Romeo (http://www.sherpa.ac.uk/romeo.php) where you can easily find an up-to-date summary of permissions that are normally given as part of each publisher's copyright transfer agreement.

As a general rule, from the editors' side, it is highly recommended to include a *copyright notice* in every published work, although it is not mandatory to claim copyright. Such a copyright notice is represented by the symbol © followed by the year of the first publication of the work and the name of the copyright holder (i.e. © Istituto Superiore di Sanità, 2007); it informs the public that the work is protected by copyright, identifies the copyright owner, and prevents possible damages that the copyright owner might otherwise receive.

From the authors' side, it is highly recommended to always ask and receive written permission from the copyright owner before using any intellectual work of others for publication, or otherwise be sure that such work is copyright free; which is the case, for example, of some government publications and laws or the works produced under the Creative Commons (CC) licenses. Such new licences represented by CC (http://creativecommons.org/) enable copyright holders to grant some or all of their rights to the public with the aim of avoiding the restrictions that most copyright laws create for the sharing of information (their motto being, from 'All Rights Reserved' to 'Some Rights Reserved').

It is important to stress that the online availability does not mean that a document is not protected by copyright. Furthermore, whenever the work of others is used, even in oral presentations in conferences or workshops, full credit of the source must be given. In written works, besides the acknowledgement of the source, the notice of the permission granted by the publisher, if any, must be included. In some cases, royalties are asked for reproduction. When receiving a manuscript for publication, editors require any necessary permission for the use of content within the manuscript that is not the author's own.

How to ask permission to reproduce published material

First of all check if it is appropriate to ask permission to reproduce published material, or if the publisher already states (in the journal, book, or its website) that published material can be freely utilized, provided that full credit of the source is included. There is generally a section called 'Permissions' including all copyright information.

In all doubtful cases, you, as authors, should write to ask permission. The letter should be addressed to the copyright owner of the book or journal where the material you wish to reproduce is published.

The e-mail address of the copyright owner is generally available in the publisher website. If no e-mail address is available, look inside the journal or the book to find the publisher's address. This is just a general scheme of a sample text to be adjusted according to your specific purposes.

Sample text for asking permission to reproduce published material

RE. Permission to reproduce published material

I would like to ask you the permission to reproduce ... (figures, tables, etc.) X appearing

- in the book indicate *title, authors, publication, and page* where the figure appears
- in the article indicate *article title, authors, journal title, issue number, pages and the year of publication.*

This material will be reproduced in the book/journal (give full details) that is to be published (indicate the date) in print/online provided that full credit of the source will be given.

If appropriate state that it is a non-profit publication, edited by _____ (this may prevent you from paying royalties).

Do not forget to indicate all contact details and give some background information.

In some cases the copyright owner will grant use of the published material without restrictions; in others, you will have to pay royalties. If you do not wish to pay royalties you may decide to describe the figure (or other material) and give full bibliographic details without reproducing it.

Some publishers may grant permission provided that you receive the same permission also from the authors of the publication; this may be more difficult to obtain and time consuming. In other cases permission may be given only for the paper version and not for the online.

3

The writing process: technical considerations

Enjoyable and effective writing is the result of a difficult balance between personalization and standardization of reliable and quality information. There is no doubt that standards facilitate communication, but good content is the prerequisite of any valuable communication.

When talking of professional literature, readers require information that is useful to them, simple to be understood, pleasant to read and easy to remember. As a general rule, you should be able to tell a story that is interesting and somewhat challenging so as to involve readers and keep their interest alert; this story will include the original elements that make it a good and relevant professional paper in respect of existing editorial rules.

Librarians spend much of their time processing and retrieving information produced by others: some documents are easy to identify and retrieve; others may make them feel puzzled for lack of basic bibliographic elements, or because such information is not placed in the right position in the document. As readers we require high standards in the presentation of any intellectual content, but when we (librarians) become writers, we often forget how important it is to organize information in a text and give the appropriate credits. On the other hand, also editors and reviewers spend much of their time reading manuscripts, and therefore appreciate receiving documents that are easy to read and edit.

The first step: reflecting on the title

The title of any document is the first step in defining its contents. Authors should establish the title of their work before developing a manuscript because it helps them to fix on its aims and intended audience as well. Of course, the title can be modified in the following stages of document production, before submitting your manuscript, and editors may suggest a different title, yet its definition in the early stages represents an important guide to help authors follow the right track.

The title is the first element to catch editors' and readers' interest and influence their decision whether or not to go on reading the document. However, always be honest and do not say in a title more than what the content of your work really is.

Titles are the most read part of any document (followed by abstract, introduction and conclusions) and also represent the first key for retrieval as they are indexed by databases and search engines of different types. The title will be included in list of references of other works, and, if appropriate, will attract more readers.

For all these reasons, the correct definition of the title is essential for any work. Therefore, it is important to select essential and descriptive words to reach the intended audience, capture their interest and be read. Make the title simple, clear, and at the same time, appealing. Long titles do not attract, at least initially, because readers are generally lazy or go in a hurry, especially if they have to select among many titles. The first words have a special meaning: they are the keys to go on reading and appreciate what comes next. Furthermore, long titles are not generally useful and will not be remembered; it is much better and effective to be concise, avoid redundancy and use simple words. Titles should not include abbreviations or acronyms.

How to write a professional paper

The steps to write a professional paper can be summarized as follows, although, according to the type and urgency of publication and other incidental situations some steps may be jumped and others added. For example, if you are invited to write a paper on a given topic, the message, target and type of publication are already set by the editor, or if you have limited time, draft should rapidly circulate for comments and no delay can be accepted.

Standard procedure to write a paper

The following steps represent a standard procedure applicable in most situations.

- Define the key message and target audience.
- Agree on the writing group.
- Search the literature.
- Define a title, prepare an outline and circulate it for comments (informal review).
- Write the first draft considering the instructions to authors.
- Circulate the draft for comments until consensus is reached among the writing group.
- Get approval to submit the paper (by the institution where you work, or sponsor).
- Submit the paper with the required stuff (cover letter, permissions, disclosures of conflicts of interest, etc.).
- Receive editor's and reviewers' comments.
- Respond to comments.
- Receive acceptance by the editor.

- Check proofs.
- Receive publication.

Each step involves a number of activities that need a proper organization and often require much unexpected time to be carried on. For example, obtaining permission for reproducing figures and tables may be sometimes very slow, as well as receiving comments from reviewers, or getting figures professionally drawn, or references duly completed. Furthermore, writing with a large group of authors is more time consuming than writing with a small group who can more easily meet and reach consensus on debated topics. Sometimes, the priority assigned to publication may be different for each individual taking part in the project and, under some circumstances, collaboration may be difficult; for example, when the leadership of the group is not clear and there are differing opinions at stake.

We should now consider the main elements associated to the production of a journal article, a book and a conference paper. From an editorial point of view, the major differences among them are related to the review process, document structure and length, while other technical characteristics such as those regarding illustrations, style, and reference format apply to any document regardless of their type. For these reasons, illustrations and references are presented as separate sections in this book (Chapters 7 and 8) as they contain suggestions that equally apply to any document regardless of their type.

Defining a sound structure is fundamental for any document, including PowerPoint presentations, posters or leaflets, because structure (be it typographical or visual) helps to understand the content of the document and also contributes to increase availability and usability in the Internet; in fact a well structured document may be simply converted into XML to allow advanced search facilities in its specific parts such as title, abstract, introduction, conclusions, and citations.

Finally, whenever you submit a paper for publication, it is important to prepare a clear and convincing letter explaining your reasons why it is important to have it published.

Paper versus non-paper documents

Today, many documents are available online; most of them still follow the traditional scheme that for centuries has been governing print production (PDF format allowing the sequential reading); others are available only in digital format and require the application of digital rules. Furthermore, while the print world has been traditionally relying on professional editors, today many digital documents can be produced with limited professional support and even without professional publishers.

To guarantee consistency in presentation, it is important to consider that there are still many rules in common to print and non-print documents, as well as some print specific and non-print specific ones: a sound document structure is fundamental to both print and non-print documents, but in the digital only documents a poor structure may more easily prevent the reading of important sections. Digital documents are read online following hypertextual links; therefore, it is fundamental to carefully define each hierarchical level and links within (and also outside) the text. The possibility to follow a personal reading path when approaching a digital document now seems obvious to most of us, but it is less evident or often under estimated when we have to make our own project for a digital only document.

For example, if it is advisable in a paper document to begin each major section on a new page, then in the digital environment each major section should be defined in a way that is easy to recognize and access through hyperlinks.

In digital-only documents it is important to reflect and decide which figure or table is so essential as to better appear in the text and which ones, instead, should be better linked to the text as they provide supplementary and not basic information. As regards visual material, whenever possible, a table or figure should be better included in one single page in a paper document, and in one screen, in the corresponding digital document, thus taking into consideration the possible variations found in viewing items through different browsers on the web. If you are not an expert, and wish to produce a document yourself for internet dissemination, it is better to always ask for an expert's advice.

4

Writing a journal article

Journal articles represent the preferred way to participate in a scientific debate on specific subjects. In any field of activity there are different types of journals characterized by a number of attributes such as scope, mission, editorial boards, review process, language, inclusion in databases, impact factor, online availability, etc. Each journal has its own 'identity card' (see box below) showing basic information not only for possible authors, but also for any person interested in the journal itself, to be properly informed on its aims and position in the national and international editorial scenario.

> **Journal identity card**
> Title
> Aims, scope and readership
> Editorial Board
> Publisher
> Frequency
> Impact factor (if any)
> Inclusion in databases
> ISSN
> Online availability
> Subscription price
> Copyright policy

Today it is not difficult to find all such information on journal websites that generally also contain more or less detailed 'Instructions to authors' and useful links to guide authors in the writing of their papers. If you decide to publish a journal article, you should consider that you are not completely free to organize information as you wish, that is as it would be in a document produced by yourself. This means that while maintaining the originality of your ideas, you have to follow a given scheme; your manuscript is subject to review and you may be asked to modify it in some parts, or it may even be rejected if not appropriate. Furthermore, you have to respect format and style rules given by the editors. Page layout is established by the journal and you do not have the possibility to change it. Once the manuscript is accepted for publication (that is when its final version is approved by the editor), you will receive proofs where you can make only essential corrections.

How to select the right journal

When you have a good idea and you wish to spread it through a journal article, the selection of the right journal is very important. In fact, supposing that you have a valuable contribution to submit, it may be accepted by one journal and refused by another one, only due to the characteristics of the journal itself.

Some small journals may be short of papers and, therefore, more prone to accept contributions, possibly also without a severe review process; others, the most prestigious international journals receiving many submissions per week, follow different selection criteria and have very high rejection rates (some even reaching 90% rejection rate). Some journals publish acceptance rates on their websites, so that you should not be too discouraged by the rejection of a paper submitted to a prestigious journal. On the other hand, acceptance from a smaller journal implies a different value of your paper in terms of perceived quality and prestige, which does not affect its intrinsic quality.

Authors cannot submit a paper to more than one journal simultaneously but if a journal rejects a paper, then it may be sent to another journal. Of course this implies a waste of time for publication.

Some authors base their choice on the value of the impact factor of the journal because the publication in those journals will guarantee better opportunities for their careers. Indeed today the number of citations received per article is a much more valid quality measure than journal impact factor and it is being used much more frequently for career advancement than in the past.

However, what is the right journal is always difficult to say. Someone would state that the right journal to publish an article is to be chosen among the ones you regularly read to be updated in your professional field. This guarantees the perfect knowledge of the subjects covered by the journal. When you become an affectionate reader, it is because you recognize the value of a journal in terms information offer, article quality, content organization, internal structure, readability, layout, etc. The same journals you regularly read may be the best to submit your paper.

Considering the extraordinarily large information offer, it is common practice that we select two or three preferred journals that we *regularly* read; generally they are the same journals that also our colleagues read, or that our senior library managers recommend for professional updating.

Sometimes it may be convenient for young or inexperienced authors to write their first articles together with senior colleagues; they will have a lot to learn from them and the best way is learning by doing. The collaboration (as authors) with well known librarians—that is people who have already published papers or took an active part in relevant meetings—may give you the opportunity to grow professionally, and at the same time build up a curriculum and acquire prestige in the professional community.

If you are not supported by an experts' advice, it may be advisable to select a low rejection rate journal as a good starting point to publish a paper. Ask advice from your supervisors even if they do not share authorship with you; also, you will have a lot to learn from the referees' comments, and shortly become strong enough to apply for more prestigious journals, if appropriate.

If you wish to publish in an open access journal, it may be useful to select a title in the Directory of Open Access Journals (http://www.doaj.org), including an ever-increasing number of journals in different fields: at the date of January 2008 there were 80 journals in the field of 'Library and Information Science' and 51 under 'Media and Communication' (you may now check the directory to evaluate the constant increase, the total number of journals currently being 3032!).

If you wish to consider the prestigious impact factor journals, go to ISI Thompson website http://scientific. thomson.com and search the Social Science Citation Index for journals following under the category 'Information Science & and Library science' (at present they are 61). All journals included in ISI databases have passed a very rigorous selection process and fight to maintain a high impact factor so they are very selective in the acceptance of articles to be published.

In any case, if you have written a document that you believe it is worth circulating online (even before the publication process), the easiest way is to deposit it in a digital archive: E-LIS (http://eprints.rclis.org/), the E-prints in Library and Information science is the best for that sector (it now contains almost 7000 documents). Most publishers allow authors to deposit their papers in digital archives before or after publication, but it is advisable to check editorial policy before submitting any document.

Instructions to authors, your first guide to write an article

Reading the 'Instructions to authors' is the first step before writing a paper to check the appropriateness of the journal scope against the content of the article you wish to write, the types of possible contributions (article, brief note, viewpoint, etc.), its length, recommended structure, reference format, etc.

Instructions must be verified repeatedly at different stages, before writing a paper, during the writing process and also after finishing your work before submitting it because many important details may often be disregarded. There are sites grouping together 'Instructions to authors' in specific fields. For example, from http://mulford.mco.edu/instr/ you can easily reach instructions to authors for over 3500 journals in the health and life sciences. This may help authors in the selection of the appropriate journal where to publish an article.

Authors following valuable instructions are guided to write a formally correct publication and are somewhat 'obliged' to adjust their texts to recommended standards. In this respect, the quality of instructions to authors may be an indicator of the quality of a journal itself. Valuable instructions should be available online and easily printed, as a whole document, as they represent a reference tool in manuscript preparation (online hyper-textual reading is not always appropriate for this purpose). Good instructions generally provide indications on the important elements having a specific 'burden' in the editorial process. Details depend on the editorial policy of the journal. Sound instructions should provide the answers to the following questions.

Which contributions are allowed?

The indication of the type of accepted contributions allows the author selecting the best editorial format suitable to his/her work: research articles, reviews, letters, short notes, briefings, commentaries, reports of meeting, viewpoints, etc. Generally, the accepted length for each contribution is also indicated. As regards editorials, in most cases, they are not accepted unless they are solicited by the editors. Sometimes also the journal sections where a manuscript may be included are indicated. According to the journal organization there might be different editors for each section to whom address the manuscript. An average length of the text is generally indicated for each type of contribution being of help both to authors and editors. When in doubt, before starting to write, it is advisable to address the journal editor to ask whether a certain type of contribution (indicating format and content) will be of interest to the journal.

Which elements should be included in title page?

This page should include the title of the article (generally as concise and informative as possible), the names of the authors and their institutional affiliation. Some journals also publish the authors' academic degree. Usually the e-mail address, phone and fax number, and possibly the mail address of the corresponding author are requested separately as well as a brief autobiographical note of each author. Some journals request also to indicate a running head (short title), the number of figures and tables included in the text and the words count. Of course all such information will not be printed as such, but will be properly organized by the editors, according to the journal layout.

Which is the recommended article structure?

As regards article structure, each field of activity follows its own traditions coming from agreed upon rules, conventions or fashions that may also be revised and changed in time.

In general, the text should be organized according to a given structure starting with an Introduction going to separate sections dealing with the different items considered in the paper and ending with Conclusions or Recommendations. If appropriate, the text may be followed by acknowledgements or annexes.

The typical structure of a scientific article is the so-called IMRAD structure that is based on the organization of elements into: Introduction, Materials and methods, Results And Discussion (IMRAD is the acronym of this structure). According to this structure, the presentation of scientific data follows a logical path that readers are accustomed to read to quickly retrieve information. This structure helps a lot to organize ideas and data into a logical sequence. In other areas the IMRAD structure may not be appropriate; yet, regardless of the field of knowledge it is always highly advisable to organize the text in separate sections that allow easier understanding and better readability. The inclusion of titles and subtitles not only provides readers with an easier approach to the text, but it also helps authors to give a major focus to explain their ideas.

Should the abstract and keywords be included?

The inclusion of an abstract is highly recommended in any professional journal. It may be in the original language of the article and also in English. It is usually of 150–200 words and should summarize the significant coverage and findings of the paper (context or background for the study, aim, main findings and conclusions or final remarks). Some journals recommend to produce a structured abstract including subheadings such as purpose, methodology/approach, findings, originality/value of the paper, etc. Sometimes structured abstracts, as well as structured articles, may help authors to include the most relevant parts of their study and present data and information in logical sequence.

The inclusion of keywords is also highly recommended in most Instructions to authors as an important element to facilitate retrieving of the articles, as librarians perfectly know. Some journals also recommend using terms from specific subject lists, such as the MESH (MEdical Subject Headings) in the biomedical field representing the controlled terms used by the National Library of Medicine in the USA, producing MEDLARS, the most important database of the field.

How should tables and figures be organized?

Technical details on how to present data in tables or figures are always given to avoid rejection of useless material. Usually, tables and figures should be proportionate to the length of the text, be informative and relevant, and be presented on separate sheets or files. Some journals specify the number of accepted tables or figures per article. The place where they are to be inserted in the text should be indicated clearly. (For detailed information on tables and figures see the Chapter 7 of this book.)

Which is the reference style?

The recommended reference style should be reported in the Instructions for authors, sometimes followed by examples of references for the most important document types (articles, books, chapter in books, etc.). (See Chapter 8 on references.)

Which is the review process followed by the journal?

The policy of review or peer review (blind/double-blind, open) is often clearly stated in instructions to authors. This is important to avoid any possible misconduct or misunderstanding by authors, reviewers (they too have to follow instructions to review manuscripts) or editors. Providing information on review procedures is fair and helps to reduce bias in publication.

How should a manuscript be submitted?

Instructions to authors also give details on how to submit a manuscript. Authors are now generally encouraged to submit their papers electronically as e-mail attachments, yet some journals still require two or three paper copies. Some journals may require an electronic submission using a given format, including separate fields for title, authors, affiliations, abstract, text, etc.; yet, in general, authors are not required to format their texts because the journal will apply their house style. The name and address of the person to whom the manuscript should be sent for submission (editor in chief, member of the editorial board, editorial secretary, etc.) as well as the managing and advertising editors may be indicated in the instructions, when appropriate, to avoid any confusion and waste of time in addressing the manuscript.

5

Writing a book, a report or a chapter therein

Writing a book is a much different commitment than writing an article, not only due to the extension of the text that is included in a book. We are not talking here about writing fiction that would require different strategies, being the world of imagination and leisure writing so diverse from the 'scientific' world. Yet, even professionally speaking, a book must tell a story that is interesting to read and, above all, useful for target readers.

Books represent an ideal format for both education and entertainment. If you accept the challenge to write a professional book, you should be aware that you need an original and quality content that has significance for the intended audience; that your proposal will be evaluated at different levels, before and also after its publication: it may also be rejected due to different reasons, not only associated to its internal quality but possibly also to the lack of marketing power, reduced budget, overproduction of books in that area, etc. And even after publication, your book may be subject to harsh criticism by the professional community and negative reviews. So, ahead of any plan, it is fundamental to evaluate the pros and cons of such a difficult and time-consuming enterprise.

Before thinking of a book proposal to an editor, you must be convinced that your book will be useful and share your conviction with your closest colleagues, with an open mind to accept suggestions and criticism. Usually the hardest critics help much more than a positive appreciation without any comment. Then, you must be aware of existing rules and you will not be surprised that despite the differences in shape, volume, work organization, etc., many editorial principles equally apply to both journals and books writing.

Why write a book?

The possible answers to this question is either that *you have been asked* by an editor, your boss, a colleague, or you terribly love writing, have lots of ideas, great enthusiasm and much time at your disposal. Generally it is much rarer today the case of a librarian deciding to write a book without external solicitation. More often you may be asked to write a book or participate in a book project by writing a chapter in a book. In these cases, you should not be concerned in defining its subject matter, and propose it to an editor as it is clear that if they asked you to write on a given topic, they are interested to have it published. Yet, you should always decide whether it is worth accepting the offer, and ask yourself questions like these, before reflecting on the best organization of the information you intend to spread:

- Do you believe it is important to write on the proposed subject?
- Are you the right person to write on that matter?
- Is it convenient for you and your career to write it?
- Do you know the publisher/editor?
- Why do you think they asked you to write?
- Are there any competing interests?

- Will you use or recommend the book in your professional activities?

- Is the suggested length of the book (or assigned chapter) appropriate to properly cover the requested topic?

- Can you estimate how long it will take you to write it?

- Is the envisaged publication schedule appropriate for your commitments?

Once you get the right answers to all these questions, you can more easily take your final decision whether to accept the offer and then sign a publication agreement.

It is different when it is you who are proposing something that has not been requested beforehand; under such circumstances, you should very carefully evaluate the pros and cons of a possible publication under different points of view, before submitting it to an editor, a publisher, or your boss. Possible questions to help you deciding may be:

- Will the book be useful to the intended target?

- Are there similar books recently published on that matter?

- Can you select the right publisher that may be interested to your work?

- Can you make your objectives clear and understandable in a couple of sentences?

- Why would it be convenient for them and for you to publish this book?

- Which is the originality of the work?

- Why is it important to get it published?

- Which is the intended audience?

- Will you use or recommend the book in your professional activities?

- Are there any competing interests?
- Can you estimate how long it will take to write it?
- Will you be able to cope with your daily library activities and at the same time write a book?

In some cases, you may have the opportunity to have a book or more likely a report published inside the same organization where you work (university, governmental agency, research institute, etc.), by an internal press or within an institutional series of publications. In some cases it may be convenient to publish an e-book, only. Some institutions may have an editorial office dealing with publications and issuing monographs or other kinds of non-commercial documents (such as technical reports, conference proceedings, booklets, or leaflets of different size and length) and these may host library and documentation studies. Before looking for an external editor, it may be useful to check the possibility to have a research published inside your institution; the staff of the publication unit, if any, will give you good advice on the best way to spread information that is considered useful and economically feasible. If production costs directly fall on to you or your institution, it is advisable to ask for more than one quote before deciding it is also important to carefully evaluate the type of paper that much influences the price as well as colour prints. Remember that the number of copies also directly affects the total price: the more copies you print, the less you pay per copy. (See also Chapter 10.)

Which part are you going to play?

Whether you will be the only author of a book or you will write it together with other authors (co-authors), or if you agree to participate in a book project by writing only one or more chapters, it is important to define beforehand the aims, scope, target and structure of the book as a whole. In this respect, it is recommended to set a draft structure indicating the main sections and to have a clear idea of the logical sequence of the issues that will be included. In the case of a book organized in chapters written by different authors, there will be an editor (or more than one editor) who will take the responsibility of the entire book and act as the co-ordinator of the project. Editors will guarantee a correct balance of the different chapters, revise the entire content to assure quality, consistency, integrity, uniformity, lack of duplications, respect of editorial standards, etc.

How to organize a sound structure

Authors and editors (in case of collective works) are responsible for the book structure that is the correct organization of information therein included. Ideas should be presented in a well balanced sequence using headings and subheadings to organize them into manageable sections and call attention on the main topics. The structure depends on the type of document you are writing (monographs on specific themes, textbooks, technical or research reports, conference proceedings, etc). A handbook, for example, may require different hierarchical levels to point out relationships among topics, from the most general to the most detailed, conference proceedings will be organized according to the conference programme, etc.

Working on structure helps authors to clarify their ideas and find the best way of presenting them. The final draft is always very different from the initial draft of a book that often includes many details (which are then deleted) in an order that is not the final one.

Divisions and subdivisions in a text can be highlighted either by using different fonts, character sizes or styles (typographical hierarchy) or by using decimal numbering to indicate relationships (numerical hierarchy). If you are editing a book yourself, you can set a style for each level; if your book will be published by an editor, they will set their own style rules, but it is always the author who suggests divisions and subdivisions of its text.

Technology may help you a lot to organize information by showing the map of the document you are writing, provided that you apply the correct style to each part of the text. In this way it is much easier to check the right position assigned to each topic and eventually modify the structure of the document.

Editors may provide authors with instructions on how to prepare a book, and authors should revise their text carefully and repeatedly check that all requirements are accomplished before submitting any proposal.

There are cases in which editors request a *camera ready copy*, which means that your manuscript should be submitted ready to be printed; in the past, it meant ready to be photographed and turned into plates for offset printing, now it may apply also to electronic documents that editors require ready to be printed, that is ready to be sent to a high-resolution laser printer or to a special device that can generate plates directly from electronic elements rather than from photographs.

Today many non-commercial organizations issuing books or reports ask authors to provide them a file to be printed or made available through the Internet. In such cases, the authors should receive detailed instructions providing basic editorial principles and a standard book or report structure to be used to write the text. In cases of doubt, it is advisable to ask the editor for clarification.

The revisions that you will undergo before reaching its final shape depend on the organization of the issuing organization or publisher; sometimes there may be a strict editorial revision, others only minor changes may be asked; sometimes a document may be deposited without revision in a digital archive or made available through the institutional website.

In this changing context, authors' responsibility in publishing documents increases a lot; in fact the useful and sometimes unique editorial support granted by the more traditional editorial process may often lack or be extremely reduced. In such cases authors should be aware of the editorial and ethical responsibilities they have in issuing a document and include the essential elements to make it editorially correct. A general check in structure regards the following items:

- Title page (including the name and logo of the institution, title of the publication, name and affiliations of authors, date and place of publication),

- Back of the title page (generally including the abstract in original language and/or in English; copyright indications),

- Table of contents (if the document is not very short),

- Lists of acronyms, abbreviations, etc, (if appropriate),

- Preface, if any,

- Introduction (explaining the background and aims of the work),

- Sequence of Sections: 1, 2, 3, etc. (which may be subdivided into different levels and represent the core information of the document),

- Conclusions or final remarks (briefly stating the results of the study, research, etc.),

- References (list of works cited in the study),

- Appendices, if any (containing supplementary material),

- Indices, if any (providing extra keys to the information contained in the document).

Balance should be guaranteed among the different component parts: the Introduction should not be too long; each section should have a similar number of pages; references within the text should follow the same uniform style.

Sometimes it may be useful to add an index that is, an alphabetical list of the main contents or items appearing in a book (such as personal or geographical names, or other topics). Indices are useful tools for long texts that can be also consulted not in sequence. They represent an added value for the best exploitation of a document. In conference proceedings an authors' index is extremely useful. Word processing programs offer today a valid support for index making, but they never replace the intellectual activity behind the creation of an index.

As regards tables and figures, be sure they are necessary to the understanding of the text, that they are original (or that authorization is received for their reproduction) and of good quality for printing. For details see Chapter 7.

As regards reference style and use in a book, you can organize them according to different criteria: each chapter may have its own references or they may appear at the end of the document in a given order (by subject, chapter, alphabetically, etc.). For details on references see Chapter 8.

Some tables or figures or other additional material that are necessary for completeness, but would interrupt the flow of reading if inserted in the text may be included in appendices at the end of the book.

Cover and title page

If you are publishing a book with a commercial editor, you will not be directly involved in the project of the cover and title page, although editors may show you the draft that will comply with their own editorial line.

On the contrary, if you are preparing a book or more likely a report for non-commercial or informal distribution, you should be sure of any legal requirement and be aware of the elements to be included in the cover or title page, that are:

- logo and name of the institution where you work (provided that you received approval for that),

- title (better if clear, concise and descriptive, see Chapter 3),

- authors or editors names,

- affiliations (generally not reported in the cover, but in the title page),

- publication date and place (if not appearing elsewhere),

- identification codes and title of the series (if any).

Sometimes, when documents are distributed only online the cover may be replaced by the title page.

Indexing

Although today it is rather easy to search words in digital documents, a well conceived index is still a useful tool for many documents or texts (both printed and online), especially if they are not sequentially consulted. Indexes are an added value for the best exploitation of information and should be carefully organized by the author.

They represent a list of the main contents or items appearing in a book or journal (such as personal or geographical names, subjects, or other topics) arranged in alphabetical order.

The choice among possible indices depends on the type of document: in a journal an authors' or subject index may be very useful (it is generally done by editors at the end of a publication year); in conference proceedings, an authors' index is always recommended; in a handbook an analytical one would be the best.

6

Writing conference papers and issuing proceedings

The major difficulty in dealing with the production of conference proceedings (representing the collection of papers presented at a conference) or abstract books (collection of the abstracts of the papers to be presented at a conference) is that it is necessary to manage works written by different persons; therefore, it is not always easy to keep with set schedules and at the same time guarantee the production of a uniform volume, suitable for publication. In most cases, conference papers are not commercially printed and distributed: this means that you should organize the entire work flow leading to the publication with limited technical support and limited resources.

If you are on the organizational side of conference proceedings, or abstract books you should have to deal with:

- the conference organizing and scientific committees,
- the conference speakers/authors of the papers/abstracts to be published,
- the editors of the conference proceedings/abstract book,
- reviewers/technical reviewers/secretarial staff,
- publishers/printers.

Energy and commitment required to produce conference proceedings or abstract books are often underevaluated, mainly because such efforts most often overlap to routine activities that cannot be disregarded; the same persons frequently play different roles as organizers, editors and authors of conference proceedings or abstract books.

- As *organizers* of an important event you may be involved in logistic decisions and scientific responsibilities as well in the selection of papers and programme definition (see Chapter 11).

- As *editors* you should check content of each contribution, define editorial rules (style, formats, length, etc.), set editorial rules and schedules and provide that they all are fully respected.

- As *authors* you may respond to a 'call for papers' or an invitation to present a paper, and write an abstract or a paper according to the instructions to authors.

Each role may be challenging, exciting and tricky at the same time.

Here follows some useful questions to reflect on the main responsibilities associated with the production of a conference paper or conference abstract book/proceedings.

What are you expected to do as an author?

As regards your involvement as a speaker in a conference and, therefore, as an author or co-author of a conference paper, before deciding whether to send any proposal (generally an abstract is required for selection within a given date), it is important to carefully evaluate the scope and aims of the conference, just as you would carefully evaluate the scope and aims of a journal before submitting an article for publication. So, you should reflect on the following questions.

- Do the conference themes really fall within your professional interests?

- Do you know some of the members of the scientific committees or invited speakers?

- Are there involved relevant people in the field?

- Is the Conference scientifically relevant for you?

- Will you be able to attend the Conference and present your paper?

- Will you have time enough to prepare a good and original work?

If you decide that it is important for you to take part in the event, then you must carefully follow the instructions given in the 'Call for papers', the first public invitation to present a contribution to the Conference. When the event is well organized, there will be instructions containing any useful detail for authors to present an abstract (format, style, number of accepted words, deadlines, contact person, etc.). Your proposal will be subject for acceptance to the evaluation of the conference committees.

Writing a Conference paper should never be underestimated. It implies a great commitment that can be somewhat compared with writing of an article in a journal: your proposal will be evaluated by the members of the scientific committees of the conference who play the part of referees and sometimes may be harsh.

In case you are an invited speaker at a conference and you did not receive detailed instructions, do not hesitate to ask any question to the organizers.

What are you expected to do as an editor?

As an editor of a volume collecting conference papers or abstracts (already selected and accepted by the scientific committee), it is fundamental that you inform authors about the deadline to receive contributions and provide that these are respected with any possible means.

It is always advisable to set such deadlines with reasonable advance of time with respect to your own schedules set to issue the volume (either in print or online): it is notorious that there may be last minute inconveniences or 'opportunity' reasons preventing to keep with schedules. On the one hand, some authors may not respect schedules and they should be repeatedly asked for that; on the other, editorial work may require unexpected long times to adjust papers to the required standards.

If you decide that the volume should be printed, and not only distributed online, you have to take agreements with the printer in advance and consider also the printer's times with reasonable flexibility to be sure that you will actually have the volume for the established date.

As editors of Conference proceedings or abstract books you should provide authors with simple and clear instructions on how to prepare their texts. The better the instructions, the easier and faster your work will be.

Which structure?

The structure of Conference Abstract books or Proceedings should reflect the conference programme following the established order of sessions. The title of the sessions should be included in the volume in the appropriate position, followed by the name and affiliation of the chairpersons.

As regards the Abstract book it is important that authors comply with the number of words required in the 'call for papers' and do not include tables, figures or references in their abstracts. Some editors may ask to prepare a structured abstract (as it happens in many scientific journals). It is advisable to include in the volume also the conference programme and an Authors' index so that the Abstract book will represent a really useful tool for all those attending the conference and need to find information quickly. When the Conference programme is included in the book, contributions may be also presented in alphabetical order. In the case of conferences that also accept posters, the abstracts referring to posters may be preceded by a different graphical sign or other mark (i.e. the letter P standing for Poster), to distinguish them from oral presentations. Sometimes posters may be grouped together at the end of the volume.

As regards Proceedings, each contribution should start on a new page and should be organized according to a uniform format (title of the conference paper, authors names and affiliations, followed by the text). Guidelines for internal subdivisions of each contribution should be established by the editors and included in the Instructions to authors containing also information on copyright, table and figures, references, etc. (see Chapters 2, 7 and 8).

In writing a conference paper all editorial rules described for journal articles or books do apply, except that the structure and, of course, length of contributions, are different. Yet, different from journal articles or books, authors of conference papers do not check proofs, thus increasing the editor's responsibility and possible mistakes. How often authors names are misspelled, affiliations not correct, and you realize it only after printing!

7

Using illustrations

The term 'illustration' includes all kinds of non-textual material (tables, graphs, maps, photographs, flowcharts, drawings, etc.) that play a significant part in the presentation of the ideas expressed in the text. Illustrations should be carefully selected and organized and at the same time be compliant with the technical requirements given by the editor; journals generally impose restrictions on the number and types of figures that you can include in a paper. Colour illustrations are costed differently in print, so they are generally not accepted or extra charges may be required. (Colour does not add extra charges in online publications.)

Illustrations summarize and emphasize key points, improve clarity, reduce narrative length; they are appealing to the reader and visually show concepts that would require many words to be explained in textual format and even so may not arrive at the same result. They are both an integral and independent part of the text. In scientific papers, non-textual material should be limited to supporting the text and be appropriate for understanding the study. In other kinds of documents, illustration may have a different evocative role not necessarily supported by the text.

When citing illustrations in the text they may defined as:

- tables (logically organized sequences of numbers or words); or

- figures (every illustrative material that is not a table, i.e. graphs or pictures).

Each illustration in a 'scientific' paper should be numbered consecutively (i.e.: table 1, figure 1) in the order of their first citation in the text, followed by a brief title (caption). They should be cited in the text and will appear soon after their citation (and not before it). Most editors require receiving illustrations as separate files as they need an editorial approach different from textual material. According to the type of publication (a magazine or newsletter is different from a scientific journal), editors may add illustrations to improve the graphical impact of the document. Illustrations included in a poster or PowerPoint presentation (see Chapter 13) follow different rules from those to be included in a printed paper.

When using a table or a figure?

Deciding what data will be presented in a table is important when planning; the same data should not be repeated in text, so authors have to choose the most appropriate format. The preference between tables or figures depends on which elements you wish to focus on: a table points out results, a graph promotes understanding of results and suggests interpretations of their meaning and relationships; graphs should be used as an alternative to tables with many entries without duplicating data in graphs and tables.

In particular, tables are used when the attention of the reader should be focused on specific data and not on trends of data. They capture information concisely, and display it efficiently; they may also provide information at any desired level of detail. Including data in table rather than in the text frequently makes it possible to reduce the length of the text.

Some technical details

A table (see the example in Figure 7.1) contains rows and columns of data that must be homogeneous among them. Each column should have a short heading guiding the reader in understanding the table content; each cell must contain data (in the case of missing data it should be indicated by special marks or letters). Internal horizontal or vertical lines are to be avoided whenever possible (editors do not generally use vertical lines to separate columns); correct spacing may be used instead to separate columns. Any necessary explanation (abbreviations, acronyms, etc.) may be given in footnotes, not in the heading. It is not convenient to have a table containing few data; in such cases it should be preferable to include data in the text.

There are many types of graphs, each one fitting specific requirements. Today it is easy to select the most appropriate graph from easy to use software, and you will immediately see how it will look like on your computer screen. Figure 7.2 shows an example of a pie chart reporting the percentage of illustrations contained in a sample set of documents in

Figure 7.1 Example of a table. Illustrations contained in a sample of documents in Library and Information Science (fictitious data)

Columns

Document type	No. pages	No. illustrations	%
Journal	85	40	9.2
Book	120	6	1.4
Conference proceedings	140	53	12.2
Technical report	90	68	15.6
Abstract book	50	1	0.2
	435	167	38.4

Rows

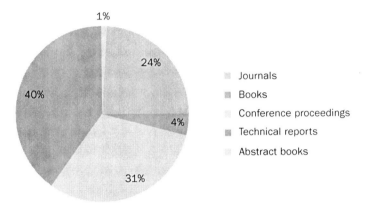

Figure 7.2 Example of a pie graph. Percentage of illustrations in different document types (fictitious data).

library and information science. It is not convenient to produce a pie chart containing many items; in such cases, a table would be preferable. Needless to say, the sum of all values reported in a pie chart should always be 100. Computer software packages help you to correct possible mistakes. All data appearing in a figure must be clearly identifiable; never forget to include legends for each item.

Figures in scientific texts should include relevant information needed for evidence, efficacy or emphasis. They should be made as self-explanatory as possible using legends, when necessary.

They should be suitable for printing (i.e. either professionally drawn and photographed, or produced as photographic quality digital prints in EPS, JPEG or GIF formats). It is always advisable to check what formats are accepted by the editor before realizing any figure that may not be utilized. Some organizations may redraw figures that are not suitable for publication, but in most cases the final printing quality depends on that of their original figures. Letters, numbers and symbols should therefore be clear and even throughout, also because figures often undergo a reduction before printing. The quality of illustrations and the use of colours should be carefully checked before sending them to the editor; also considering that for economic reasons, figures are generally printed are in black and white. Some journals publish illustrations in colour only if authors pay an extra charge.

If illustrations are taken from other published sources, permission should be obtained by the copyright owner (except for documents that are in the 'public domain') and the original source should be fully acknowledged. Many editors require evidence of permission granted to be attached to the submitted publication.

Last but not least, if photographs of people are used, either the subjects must not be identifiable or authors should obtain a written permission to use such images and supply it to the editor. It is not sufficient to hide the eyes of a subject to make it anonymous.

When placing a figure or table, check its orientation within the text so that it can be read horizontally as the text is both in print and in the online version. In some cases you may find figures or tables that follow a different orientation, but they are difficult to read. Whenever possible it is advisable to reduce the number of columns or the size of figures rather than propose an orientation different from the text.

8

Citing the work of others:
how and why

Citations included in a paper provide evidence of scholarly research and should allow the reader the opportunity to locate and check the source.

Science develops by using the work of others. There would not be any progress if we were to invent everything from scratch. Citing works that have been used in our study is at the same time ethically correct and essential to track the development of science. Today it is also possible to follow progress in research by coupling references to the same source. Furthermore, citations received give a valuable indication of the impact and use of a study or research, and at present it is rather common to link references among them and track the development of a study.

A bibliography is the list of references cited in a text and it is normally located at the end of your document. Producing a correct description of a reference (intended as the detailed indication of the source from which you have obtained your information, i.e. book, journal article, report, etc.) is often rather bothersome and time consuming; it requires much attention by the author and contributes to determine the quality of the work.

Editors do not generally take responsibility for the correctness of references included in a paper; therefore, it is most advisable that all cited sources should be verified directly by the authors. It is not correct to cite secondary sources of information, that is citations reported by others, which may be misleading and generate added errors, as in a domino game.

All sources directly used to prepare the text should be reported in bibliography.

Citation styles may vary according to the rules established by the editors and provided in the instructions to authors. All references and citations included in a paper should be conform to the journal's or book's style rules. What is accepted in one journal or book may not be good in another one. When instructions are not detailed enough, you may check other books or journals published by the same editors to see which reference style they follow in their publications.

Full citations generally appear at the end of the text and citations in text may be indicated by numbers (in parentheses or apex) or by author/year, as explained below.

Citations indicated by numbers

References are numbered consecutively in the order in which they are first mentioned in the text. References in the text, tables and legends are identified by Arabic numerals, as in the following example:

> As regards illustrations, attention should be placed on the autonomous role of each figure or table to be included in the text (1). You should keep in mind all rules governing the organization of the document (2–3).

The corresponding reference list should be numerically reported at the end of text, in the 'References' section, according to the editor's recommended style. The example below refers to a list of references related to the citations of the above sample text. These references are drawn up according to the *Vancouver style*.

References

1. Gustavii B. *How to write and illustrate a scientific paper.* Lund: Studentlitteratur; 2000.

2. Matthews JR, Bowen JM, Matthews RW. Successful scientific writing. A step-by-step guide for biological and medical sciences. Cambridge: Cambridge University Press; 2000.

3. Huth EJ. *How to write and publish papers in the medical sciences.* 2nd ed. Baltimore: Williams & Wilkins; 1990.

Citations indicated by author/year

References are reported with the name of the first author followed by *et al.* (if there are more than two authors) and the year of publication; in case of two authors, both should be cited with '&' between the two. For example:

> As regards illustrations, attention should be placed on the autonomous role of each figure or table to be included in the text (Gustavii 2000). You should keep in mind all rules governing the organization of the document (Matthews *et al* 2000; Huth 1990).

The references are alphabetically listed at the end of the text, in the 'References' section, as in the following example:

> Gustavii B. How to write and illustrate a scientific paper. Lund: Studentlitteratur; 2000.

> Huth EJ. How to write and publish papers in the medical sciences. 2nd ed. Baltimore: Williams & Wilkins; 1990.

Matthews JR, Bowen JM, Matthews RW. Successful scientific writing. A step-by-step guide for biological and medical sciences. Cambridge: Cambridge University Press; 2000.

To minimize errors in references, authors should verify them against the original documents.

Reference to 'Personal communication' should be avoided whenever possible because it would be difficult to retrieve; if a 'personal communication' provides essential information not available from a public source, the name of the person and date of communication should be cited in parentheses in the text.

Elements to be included in a reference

Apart from the style followed by each editor, as a general rule, each reference should include all the bibliographic elements required to identify the source unambiguously. In synthesis, the following items should be considered for a correct citation of:

- *Journal article*: Author, title of the article, journal name, year of publication, volume, issue and pages.
- *Book (or report)*: Author/editor, title of the book, place of publication, publisher (or issuing organization), year of publication, report series and/or report numbers.
- *Chapter in book*: author, title of the chapter, editor, title of the book, place of publication, publisher (or issuing organization), year of publication and pages of the chapter.

- *Conference paper*: author, title of the paper, editor, title of the proceedings, conference date and place, place of publication, publisher (or issuing organization), year of publication and pages of the paper.

When citing electronic material the bibliographic elements are always the same, but the indication of the type of electronic source should be included (e.g. CD-ROM) and the Internet address should be added for each online material preceded by 'available from' and the date of the last visit. Preference should be given to persistent links/addresses to the cited documents (citations of general websites should be avoided).

Reference styles

Reference style may be different according to specific fields of knowledge or traditions. Some fields share recommended citation standards. Before you start writing your list of references, always check which style is recommended by the editor.

In the biomedical field, for example, the *Vancouver style* is highly used. It is based on a numbered list of references. Numbers appear in the body of the text, in the appropriate position, and at the end of the text the corresponding numbered list is reported as bibliography.

Citations rules according to *Vancouver style* are available from the US National Library of Medicine (NLM) providing detailed samples of different reference citation formats in its website at http://www.nlm.nih.gov/bsd/uniform_requirements. html. As this style is used by the US National Library of Medicine that produces the MedLARS (Medical Literature Analysis and Retrieval System), the most important database in biomedicine in the world, it is practically recognized as a *de facto* standard in this field.

As for the psychological, social and behavioural sciences, the *APA style* established by the American Psychological Association is widely used (http://apastyle.apa.org); APA, based in Washington, is a scientific and professional organization that represents psychology in the United States; the *APA style* provides complete guidance on the rules of style and is a precious reference tool for all those studying and working in the social sciences.

Another widely used style is *Chicago style* (http://www .chicagomanualofstyle.org/home.html) defining it as 'the bible of the publishing and research community'. It is produced by the University of Chicago Press that has been publishing books for scholars, students and general readers since 1892. The *Chicago Manual of Style* presents two basic reference systems, the humanities style (notes and bibliography) and the author/date system. Choosing between the two often depends on subject matter and nature of sources cited, as each system is favoured by different groups of scholars. It is easy to use, and provides quick answers to style and editing questions.

Last but not least, among the most commonly used citation styles, the *Harvard style*. It is also-called the author–date style. It was developed at Harvard, USA and grew in popularity during the 1950s and 1960s, especially in the physical and natural sciences and more recently the social sciences. This system uses the author's name and date of publication in the body of the text, and the bibliography at the end of the text is given alphabetically by author.

Many professional publications often have their own house style that introduces specific variations within these general conventions. It is important to know that citing rules are not different according to the type of publication (journals, books, grey literature or others). A correct bibliography is essential in any type of publication, and also the documents distributed through the net or otherwise informally produced should follow a uniform style.

Today there are quite a few citation management software packages (such as EndNote, Reference Manager, Refworks, ProCite, etc.) allowing users to search hundreds of online library catalogues and e-resources with the purpose of creating personal reference libraries and generating bibliographies. Many researchers, writers and students now depend on these products to locate bibliographic data and create their bibliographies for curricula vitae, manuscripts, grant proposals, term papers and other publications. This software may be expensive but is very useful for the automatic creation of bibliographies and facilitate a tedious and error-prone activity when performed manually. At the same time, they can save many hours of typing and interpreting style requirements for scholarly publications by simply selecting the publication by name and generating a perfectly formatted document according to the required style.

9

Editorial revision

Editorial revision is a process that ensures that the technical content of a document is complete, accurate, and understandable to the intended audience and may largely improve the quality of the publication guaranteeing an unsuspected added value. A careful revision of any document before their diffusion is fundamental at all levels and for any type of publication, especially for those publications that do not undergo a peer-review process or any other editorial review that guarantees improvement to the original text. Editorial revision enhances quality but, the technical content of a document, be it a journal article or book, is always its most important attribute: if content is flawed, it is irrelevant that the document looks typographically perfect, has excellent design and page layout and no grammatical errors.

Generally speaking, the author is responsible for the initial revision of the text before submitting it for publication, then there may be a peer review process or any other kind of revision editing depending on the type of publication, on the editorial policy of the publisher or issuing organization, and on the budget available.

As already mentioned, peer review requires a special organization of the editorial office (see Chapter 2) to track all correspondence between editors, reviewers and authors and generally secretarial staff is needed to follow all contacts, solicit reviewers and authors to keep with schedules, etc.

In general, revision should be applied to any text before dissemination; apart from peer review, revision editing may be carried out at different levels (rush, standard or professional edit) according to specific situations. In fact, the levels of revision may be influenced by many factors such as:

- speed in diffusion (if a text needs to be urgently spread, revision will be necessarily limited to the essential elements),

- availability of specialized editorial staff (if it is possible to rely on expert editorial advise or collaboration, it is always advisable to do so),

- budget (if it is possible to pay for professional editorial or language revision, in case of texts written by non-native speakers, it is always advisable to do that).

Attention to details increases at each revision level taking into account the following elements:

- *Policy.* The document must not be in contrast with aims and scope of the issuing organization; copyright must be respected; unnecessary promotion of specific commercial products should be avoided; no human or animal rights should be infringed.

- *Technical content.* The document must be coherent, consistent and balanced in each part, all cited tables and figures should be included and be correct.

- *Copyediting.* The document should be revised in its language, grammar, format and style: typos and spelling errors; garbled passages; format inconsistency; dropped lines and words, etc.

If you are in a hurry, and you cannot rely on external collaborations, it is fundamental to reflect on 'policy' issues and then just look at the basic structure of the text, possible inconsistencies, verify the inclusion of all tables and figures that have been cited, etc. In any case, read the text over and over again from the beginning to the end before releasing it and, if possible, have it read by some closer colleague or friend that will surely be able to notice some faults that you were not able to see. It should be advisable to take a psychological distance from your text, leave it waiting for a while and then read it again, or let it be read by somebody else before its diffusion. You will be surprised to discover that it is not as perfect as initially you believed!

From my experience as a technical editor, I can say that most authors are in love with their text and they are convinced that it is absolutely faultless; they are not initially willing to accept suggestions with a positive attitude as they are convinced that their work is perfect, but the kind support of technical editors helps them recognize that the 'perfect creature' may have some faults; in the final revision stage of the editorial process, most authors are very grateful to editors for their precious contribution.

Any organization responsible of issuing documents and publications (whether commercial or not, in paper copy or digital format) should be aware of the importance of revision editing, and find the best strategies to educate authors to produce editorially correct documents (provide training courses, informal meeting, individual assistance, etc.). Instructions to authors should always be available as a useful guide to make authors aware of existing editorial rules and help them tailor the document in the most autonomous way.

Editors or issuing organizations often provide a checklist to help authors in the production of a correct document. Some typical questions in the checklist include:

- Are all the essential elements included in the text?
- Are all the tables or figures cited in the text included?

- Are all the references complete?
- Are copyright transfer documents signed?
- Are permissions to reproduce figures or tables from other publications attached?
- Are the units of measure (length, height, weight, volume, etc.) standardized?
- Do they follow the International System (SI) for measurements?
- Are decimal multiples correct and uniform?

How to handle proofs

Proofs represent a final stage of the publication process when authors can check the layout of their paper (including tables and figures), after completion of the review process, and following any adjustments made by the editors according to the house style. Proofs may contain some requests by editors that should be carefully answered.

Authors receiving proofs are asked to check the text very quickly to prevent delays in publication and send them back, duly signed with 'approval to print'. Today proofs are generally sent by e-mail (in PDF), but be careful to follow instructions on how to send them back: some editors may ask to send a fax with corrections, others an e-mail, or, more rarely to correct the file. In the case of multiple authors only the corresponding author will receive proofs and will be responsible to sign them.

At this stage authors cannot make any substantial change, but just correct typographical errors, or major mistakes that would crucially damage the publication. If you believe that important changes are still necessary, it is advisable to contact the editors to explain your reasons with the objective to reach an agreement on modification.

Proofs should be read word by word (better if more than one person can read them) without giving anything for granted, because also the most prestigious editors may commit mistakes, especially if graphs or pictures are re-drawn from the original ones received by the authors.

When correcting proofs, use a very clear handwriting to be sure that your corrections will be understood. It should be advisable to use conventional marks for proof-reading, that you can easily find also in the internet. Just include in the search engine 'proof correction marks' and you will find many examples, i.e.:

- http://www.cse.dmu.ac.uk/~bstahl/CORRECTION_MARKS.pdf
- http://www.ideography.co.uk/proof/marks.html
- http://intl.elsevierhealth.com/authorguide/corr_marks.cfm (The corrections marks are not reproduced here for copyright reasons!)

The general concept for correcting proofs is that you mark the wrong letter with a mark and use the same mark in the margin of your sheet, followed by the correct letter. In any case, even if you do not use conventional marks be sure that you do not create confusion and possible misinterpretation.

10

Producing leaflets

Leaflets may represent a valuable communication tool in libraries. They may have different aims: educate, inform, draw attention, offer services, search for collaboration, etc. and can be used and re-used on different occasions: events, exhibitions, fairs, conferences, library desks, as an attachment to journals, books, letters, etc. Furthermore, a leaflet is a portable tool that can be read as a reminder of an activity or message.

Once you have pondered on producing a leaflet and decide that it may be convenient for you and your library mission, you should carefully consider its costs including project, editorial work, paper, print and distribution. You should ask yourself:

- Who will pay for all that?
- Have you the proper skill and necessary time to produce a useful tool?
- Can you rely on external professional services or should the leaflet be in-house produced?
- Have you a set budget for that?

It is then advisable to contact one or more services or printers to ask quotations and negotiate on price.

Consider the different options that may directly influence leaflet production prices: design, paper quality, number of pages and number of copies, type of binding, etc. Furthermore, if you give the printer a PDF file ready for print it will be less expensive than if you require other editorial work.

Remember that designing a leaflet for standard paper sizes can save money, but consider also that the best quality is not associated with the most convenient price. Before making a decision, always ask to see samples of final products already realized by the service you selected and check the proposed paper, colours, print quality and ask for references.

If your budget is limited (as it often is in most libraries) and you cannot rely on professional designers or printers, you may wish to produce a leaflet by yourself. Indeed today in-house production is much easier than in the past and with a few good tips you can reach satisfactory results at very low costs.

Some hints for autonomous creation

First of all, consider that a leaflet must inform quickly (so fix on the message, be clear and limit text) and should be carried easily in a pocket or bag (so mind of its shape and size). If you are able to harmonize text, colours and images, you can also produce valuable leaflets without being an expert in the use of graphical software.

Here follow some practical tips for autonomous production:

■ *Define your target and aims.* Think of the message you wish to get across and why, then select the best way to express it in words and graphics. Leaflets are seldom read from the beginning to the end, but scanned for the most relevant information.

- *Be essential and clear.* You cannot say all, but select the right information to catch your audience.

- *Define size, shape, paper, colour and print.* All these elements are strictly interconnected. They will determine the extension of the text (how detailed you can be), and the inclusion of images and graphs. If you print the leaflet yourself, choose paper and colours that can fit your printer. If you use A4 paper (ISO sheet size, 8.27 × 11.7 inches; 221 × 297 millimetres), you can cut it after print to adjust more than one leaflet in a page, or fold it once or twice, or more, to make a booklet; you may project different sizes within the A4, keeping in mind space required for margins. You may select paper of different quality and colour (in terms of weight, thickness, brightness, etc.) for the cover and the inner pages of the booklet.

- *Sketch a layout to harmonize text and images and create a visual logic.* Keep the same graphical line in all pages of the leaflet to create harmony and assure a pleasant reading.

- *Ask for feedback* from your colleagues at different production stages and duly consider their reactions and advice.

- *Use hierarchical levels* (by using different colours, fonts, positions in the page, etc.) to point out the main concepts and mind of the role of blank spaces to help readers focus on important content. You may use clues (bullets, arrows, colours) to stress concepts.

- *Edit your text to be clear and easy to remember.* Use short paragraphs, active voice and create headings to point out concepts.

- *Select images and colours to help getting your message across.* Check their quality (at least 300 dpi, saved in JPG or TIF format file) and copyright restrictions, or create images yourself, but do not use too many colours and be careful of the background colours and artwork that may create difficulties in reading the text. Remember that heavy colours may leak from one side of the page to the other when the paper is too thin.

- *Include all important elements allowing readers to identify* who you are (name and logo of your institution), where you are (postal address and website) and how to contact you (telephone numbers and e-mail address), when the leaflet was produced (date) and by whom (printed by).

- *Get approval* and always *carefully check the final draft* before printing the all run.

- *Follow a careful distribution strategy* and use feedback for future actions.

11

How to organize a conference

More than in any other field, conference organization is an activity that is very often under-evaluated both in terms of time and effort required to carry it forward properly. It is generally inserted as an added task in routine activities; initially it only appears as a very appealing opportunity of meeting people, organizing an exciting scientific programme, exchanging new ideas with the most distinguished representatives in our fields of interest, developing new projects, participating in social events, appearing in the press, etc. All this is true, but the reverse side of a conference organization is often obscure until you are not already too deeply involved to possibly give it up: conference organization is indeed hard work that often puts you under strong pressures; it requires the capacity to cope with limited budget, the use of great diplomacy to solve inevitable conflicts, the ability of planning every activity in advance of time and solve a number of last minute 'tragedies' that often seem to go behind the limits of our responsibilities.

Conference organization is an activity that is limited in time; in fact it represents a complementary commitment that has a starting and an end point within a working routine. However, this also means that any service we are supposed to render must also be carried on properly during the period when the conference is being organized, and also while the conference is taking place there will be urgent routine services that cannot be delayed.

Indeed organizing a conference might require the commitment of a full time job, but when you work within an institution (be it a library or any other service), it is not possible to stop all other primary activities and concentrate only on the organization of an event.

Furthermore, the best way to learn how to organize a workshop or conference is experience; in fact there is no handbook good enough to teach you how to cope with the different and often unpleasant situations that you might encounter when you decide to take on the challenge to be involved in a conference. Theories are never useful when an urgent decision is required to solve a number of very practical problems, which could not have been envisaged beforehand. The most convenient solution is not always the best, but sometimes opportunity reasons represent the finest explanation for apparently weird solutions.

Therefore, before assuming any responsibility in the conference organization enterprise, it is fundamental to have a clear idea of the objectives for which the conference is organized and the roles of the different people who will take part in it.

Once you have a clear idea of what organizing a big conference means, the same principles might be very useful also to organize smaller events at local or national level.

The basic steps of conference planning can be summarized as follows:

- Define objectives and roles (conference scope, target, committees, expected results).
- Create a conference website and/or a newsletter for regular updating.

- Activate a *call for papers.*
- Select papers.
- Define the conference scientific programme.
- Define the conference social programme.
- Publish an abstract book and/or conference proceedings.

Define roles and objectives

Some conferences represent regular meetings of people belonging to the same association or a research group, or sharing the same interests in a given field. Such appointments may take place every year, or two or more years and are generally devoted to discuss a particularly relevant issue in the field. They may be planned with years in advance, take for example the Annual IFLA Conferences on specific issues:

- 2009: Title to be defined. Milan, Italy, August 2009
- 2008: 'Libraries without Borders: Navigating Towards Global Understanding', 10–15 August 2008, Québec, Canada
- 2007: 'Libraries for the future: Progress, Development and Partnerships', 19–23 August 2007, Durban, South Africa
- 2006: 'Libraries: Dynamic Engines for the Knowledge and Information Society', 20–24 August 2006, Seoul, Korea.

Other conferences arise from a more circumscribed necessity to discuss important or strategic issues having special relevance for economic, political or other reasons, for example to announce an important discovery, launch of a new project, search for collaborations, etc.

In the beginning there is a general idea of gathering people for a conference to discuss trends and opportunities. Then the pros and cons of a conference are evaluated in a restricted circle of close colleagues and friends and the idea may start circulating in discussion lists to collect further incentives to go on.

There is always a leader, or a leading group, acting as a starter to provide the first impulse before a more formal committee is established. The members of such committees may be appointed by the President of an Association, or institution having a primary role in the conference organization or by other relevant groups, or commissions playing a particularly significant part in the field considered.

In general the responsibility of the organization of a large event is shared between a *Scientific Committee* and a *Local Organizing Committee*, which are supported by a *Scientific secretariat* and/or a *Technical secretariat*. The naming of the conference committees and their size as well as number of secretarial or administrative staff involved may vary according to different situations; you might have a 'Programme Committee', or an 'Organization Committee', or a 'Management Committee' or many other different types of 'Conference boards', etc.

The scope and relevance of the event, the number of people and institutions involved, the issues at stake, the expected audience, etc. have a direct influence on the organizational structure. Yet, apart from the existence of different committees, to guarantee a successful event, it is important to be clear about what roles they play, and what responsibilities they share in the conference organization.

In some cases (i.e. in small events), the same individual persons may be play different parts. In other cases (i.e. in large international events), it would be advisable to appoint representatives of different countries representing diverse local situations and acting as local promoters of the event in each country.

As the organization of a conference requires financial support, it is also important to consider that there are organizations (e.g. institutions, private companies, banks, etc.) that may be happy to act as *conference sponsors* and receive good publicity during the different stages of the conference in exchange for their support. The sponsors' names, for example, may appear in the conference programme, on the website, in the conference folders, in the proceedings, etc., to guarantee an appropriate balance for investment given to support the conference. Sponsors may also collaborate to pay the expenses for coffee breaks or social dinners and be thanked for that, thus providing the required visibility in exchange for financial support.

In some cases, especially when resources are limited, the help of *volunteers* may become fundamental to carry on many organizational activities that require much time and energy. A conference is a perfect opportunity for students or young people to learn, contact people and professionally grow. There was a wonderful group of university students last year (2006) in Cluj-Napoca, Romania where the 10th European Association of Health Information and Libraries (EAHIL) Conference took place. They collaborated with enthusiasm with the executive staff in all organizational activities, assisting speakers and delegates for any possible requirements (from airport transfer to hotel accommodation, social dinners and tourist activities, etc.) and also taking part in the scientific activities of the conference. Of course volunteers must be properly guided and receive clear instructions to be supportive and contribute to the Conference success.

Scientific Committees and their responsibilities

Who are its members?

In the cases of small workshops or conferences there may be just one person (the conference organizer) responsible for the event who is often supported by one or more advisors; yet in cases of larger events a Scientific committee is more or less formally established and it has full responsibility of the scientific content of the conference.

The scientific committee generally consists of a group of relevant people, experts in the field and generally working in prestigious and well-known institutions. The number of the committee members may vary according to the relevance of the conference, but it is always advisable that it is odd, just in case of decisions to be taken by majority of votes.

The members of the committee may come from different countries, not only in the case of international meetings; there might be conferences of national relevance having prestigious foreign members in the scientific committee to give the event a major impact.

When selecting foreign members you should have the required budget to pay for their allowances, including expenses for pre-conference programme meetings.

In the selection of committee members attention must also be given to genre, avoiding including only males in the group, as has traditionally happened in many sectors. The same rule should apply in the selection of the chairperson for conference sessions that in the past was generally called 'Chairman', as evidence of neglecting any possible genre differentiation.

What are the working procedures?

Procedures may change according to specific situations, but in general the scientific committee meets to discuss the conference scientific organization in advance to properly define the conference objectives, schedules and rules to follow.

Although telephone contacts and different kinds of digital communication today save a lot of time without *vis á vis* communication, direct exchanges of ideas among the committee members are still essential in the first stages because it facilitates the development of new ideas. When a good understanding is established among the committee members, the following decisions or suggestions may circulate via e-mail, teleconference or through other forms of digital contacts.

E-mails definitely work, as they can share information simultaneously among all members; however, it is important not to exaggerate and circulate useless details that may distract from the actual objectives.

Attention should be given to the fact that e-mail messages—as any other form of digital information—may be easily transmitted to other people that the scientific committee may not like to be involved; this may cause some 'political' mishap and create concern. For instance, during the organization of a recent international conference, one of the *invited speakers* declined via e-mail our invitation due to other commitments and at the same time suggested the name of another colleague who, in his opinion, could perfectly take his place. The e-mail circulated outside the conference committee and other well known colleagues proposed different substitutes; a sort of virtual dispute was started about the possible 'candidates' creating a situation that required much diplomacy to be solved!

Also, we are now testing the use of blogs that can keep everybody updated on the development of the conference programme, step by step: they seem to be a valuable tool, open for comments by the entire Internet community, but there is still some scepticism about this new medium.

Another form of sharing useful information is the Google spreadsheet, which allows individual members of a group to update the same file online (provided that authorization is given). The greatest advantage of this system is that you do not duplicate files requiring constant updating, but you share the same file.

What is its role?

The main responsibility of the scientific committee is to define the policy and programme of the conference. The committee is established when the idea to organize a conference is already mature and it has been shared, discussed, supported and positively evaluated with the closest colleagues and advisors who may become part of the committee itself.

The scientific committee is fully responsible for all the scientific activities related to the conference; financial responsibilities may be assigned to other people.

The scientific committee decides whether it will be appropriate to have *invited speakers* to present a lecture at the conference, who should be invited and why; it may also decide whether to activate a *call for papers* and select the papers received as a spontaneous adhesion to the conference debate.

Invited speakers represent important personalities in the field, so their presence will give the conference the highest prestige and guarantee participation of a large audience. They may be informally asked to participate and then may receive a more formal written request. Their names may be included and circulate in the programme only after acceptance.

Invited speakers are very busy people and you must take agreements to fit their schedules in due advance. Sometimes the dates of the conference are set or postponed according to the availability of invited speakers. Even so, alas, they might have last minute commitments that prevent them taking part in the event. In the best cases they will send you a substitute who will have the saddest duty to present (in the worse cases to read!) a paper he/she does not always completely understand. It is common that the miserable substitute is obliged to afford the challenge of a PowerPoint presentation that looks very cryptic. However, when the scientific committee is not lucky enough as to have a substitute for a missing speaker, organizers may be compelled to fill a blank schedule with a prolonged discussion or accept added speakers that may not be completely reliable.

The selection of invited speakers and chairpersons is very delicate: in every sector there are unwritten rules that members of the scientific committee cannot neglect. Furthermore, there is always an important balance to maintain as regards the decision to put together, or in similar positions in the programme, people or institutions acting on the same grounds and responsibilities. Attention should also be paid to guarantee equal opportunities for women and men.

In any case, the scientific committee should be able to promptly solve any possible dispute that inevitably arises during the organization of the conference with highest level of diplomacy and flexibility at the same time.

Tips for a correct *call for papers*

A *call for papers* is a formal announce of the conference, circulating in different media, by which people interested in the issues proposed are asked to submit their abstracts for a possible communication or poster.

A *call for papers* contains the following information that represents the results of the agreement reached among the committee members:

- Conference title, place, date and logo, if any,
- Conference scope, objectives and target,
- Conference committees (names and affiliations of all members),
- Conference sessions and suggested relevant topics,
- Instructions for authors who wish to submit an abstract,
- Deadlines to submit abstracts and receive notice of acceptance/refusal,
- Contacts for information.

A brief comment on the above points will help you reflect on the multifaceted tasks of the scientific and/or organizing committees.

The *conference title* must be very carefully chosen among the committee members; it must be descriptive and easy to remember, not too long but appealing at the same time. The search for an appropriate title often stimulates creativity among committee members and helps them to define the correct meaning and target of the event. Just like it happens for the title of a journal article or book, also for conferences the choice of the effective title is fundamental for the success of the event; it greatly contributes to determine the highest level of interest and increases the number of possible speakers and participants. Also, after the conference is finished, the title will be used in the proceedings and remain as an important key to trace the event and all the associated documents, also through the Internet.

Attention must be given to the fact that there might be some similar titles that may generate confusion or priority concerns. The web now helps us a lot for this. I remember some years ago, when the Internet was not yet so helpful, we were going to organize a conference having exactly the same title as another conference organized in another country, a few days before ours. Only at the last minute we realized this inconvenience and luckily enough were able to change the title of our conference; if we did not see the other title in time, there would be great discussion on possible plagiarism and much confusion between the two events.

As regards the conference *logo*, it should be advisable to have one ready to be reproduced since the first public announcement of the conference. The logo should be designed by professional graphics and approved by the committee. There are cases when amateur designers produce very appealing logos, but improvization does not always work. The conference logo should be clearly identified as a distinctive element of the event, be original and not confused with other similar ones; it should be easy to remember for its distinctive character, even without the name of the conference; it should be 'readable' also in black and white, be clear and neat in its tracts and it should be possible to reproduce it in different sizes without loosing effectiveness. Its position in the page layout should be properly evaluated not to be confused with other elements in the page (institutional logos, or other graphs).

The choice of the *conference place*, and the evaluation of practical issues associated with it, also represents an important decision to be shared with the local organizing/administrative committees, if any, or with a representative of the place where the conference will take place. Careful consideration must be given to the logistic aspect that dramatically influences the success of the initiative. The following questions should be answered before taking the final decision:

- Is this place easy enough to reach?
- Is the conference hall large enough for the expected audience?

- Can it be granted for free or at a low price, by the institutions involved in the conference (universities, scientific bodies, etc.)?

- Is it easy to reach from the city centre?

- Are there the required conference facilities?

- Are technical equipment and software up-dated? (How sad it is to discover that the marvellous effects of a PowerPoint presentation do not work there!).

- Is there a place suitable for posters, if any?

- How expensive is it?

- Is the place also attractive for leisure activities, after the conference and/or for social events?

- Are there important (either modern or ancient) libraries to be visited or other relevant historical places or attractions not necessarily related to libraries activities?

- Does the place offer accommodation for large numbers of people and at different prices?

- Is there an agency taking the responsibility for the organizational aspects (travel and accommodation)? And is it expensive?

Take the final decision only if the number of 'yes' answers far exceeds the number of 'no', or 'I am not sure'.

The *conference date* must be studied with a calendar in hand, also considering that holidays and festivities may vary in different countries and, under some circumstances, too high or too low temperatures may represent a serious obstacle for those who are not accustomed to that climate. For some people a conference on Saturday or Sunday may be a good opportunity to participate without losing time for 'work', and take advantage of the cheapest air tickets, for others it may be seen as an added work commitment during the weekend. It is important to know traditions of different fields and places and give them the proper consideration.

Before setting the conference dates, it is advisable to be informed if there are other conferences on similar issues that might attract the interest of the same target groups. This can be achieved through a simple Internet search or through other more or less informal sources: a call to colleagues involved in similar activities or members of professional associations or other important committees in the field. In this case, it is better not to choose the same or very close dates because even if not overlapping, participants would be compelled to choose just one event, due to budgetary or organizational reasons. Take for example the Online Information Conference (http://www.online-information.co.uk/index.html), a fixed appointment for information specialists—always scheduled at the beginning of December in London—attracting delegates from many countries across all continents, and providing a forum dedicated to learning, debate, professional development, technology reviews and assessments, expert discussion as well as case-study presentations and the sharing of research results and opinion. It would be practically impossible to organize a successful event concerning libraries and information science in the same period!

As already mentioned, the *call for papers* must contain information on the *Conference scope, objective and target* as defined by the scientific committee. Although the committee may agree in principle on these issues, when writing them down to be published and spread to the world, they mysteriously seem to become obscure and much rephrasing is necessary before reaching a final consensus.

Writing defines better then speaking the limits and opportunities of any issue at stake; which is why many discussions often arise at the moment about giving the final approval to what was suggested and agreed upon only verbally.

The conference objective must be clear and credible. It is not sensible to declare an unreasonable objective, but try to convince that the conference is useful and that it will meet its objectives. The *call for papers* should contain information on the main topics to be discussed during the conference; it is not always advisable, however, to give too strict limits because important issues, initially not conceived as relevant, may then be excluded.

The names of the *conference committee* members and their affiliations will contribute to give credit and credibility to the objective declared. It is advisable to follow alphabetic order in the list of names to avoid any other concerns over priority.

Defining the titles for the *conference sessions* may help to guide the authors and committee members in the definition and selection of the contributions that better fit the conference objectives.

In the *call for papers* it is also very important to give precise *instructions for authors* who may wish to submit a paper such as:

- How to indicate the name, surname and affiliations of authors and e-mail address of correspondence author.
- For which session is the paper proposed?
- Is it intended for an oral communication or poster?
- How many words should the abstract contain? Should it be structured in pre-defined paragraphs (introduction, objectives of the study, etc.)?

Sometimes it may be convenient to provide a separate sheet with instructions to authors and/or properly arrange a conference website to submit the abstract online. It may also be convenient to provide a sample format to write an abstract, especially when they will circulate among the conference participants in print or/and online. Today there is an increasing number of free software to manage and share the entire flow online, without extra charge. See, for example, the Open Conference System (http://pkp.sfu.ca/?q=ocs), a free Web publishing tool that creates a complete Web presence for your scholarly conference. (The Open Conference System is produced within the Public Knowledge Project (http://pkp.sfu.ca/), that also makes available the free software Open Journal System to create your own electronic journal.)

In any case, the *deadline* for abstract submission should be included in a prominent position in the *call for papers* and also the date when the author should receive communication about acceptance/rejection of the proposed paper should be clearly shown.

Never forget at the end of any announcement, to give all details of the *contact person* for information on the event (e-mail, telephone, fax, postal address, etc.). And be sure that the contact person gives immediate answers for any question received. Useless to say, the conference committee members should assure that any submitted abstract does not circulate outside the conference committee before approval.

Conference fee may be also included in the first announcement as well as other logistics information, if available.

Here follows (Figure 11.1) an example of a *call for papers* for an international Conference on Open Access to scientific publications organized by the Istituto Superiore di Sanità, the National Institute of Health of Italy in 2006.

As you see in the example, all the main elements are included (conference title and place, deadlines, objectives, target, etc.). As often happens, also in this case, the logo of the conference had not been included in the first announcement; in fact it was produced later and appeared in all the following documents: second announcement, website, final programme, leaflets, posters, abstract book, proceedings, etc.

Call for papers generally circulate via e-mail and through discussion lists, blogs or forums. Sometimes they may be

Figure 11.1 Example of a first announcement of a conference

International Conference
INSTITUTIONAL ARCHIVES FOR RESEARCH:
EXPERIENCES AND PROJECTS IN OPEN ACCESS

Rome (Italy), 30 November–1 December 2006
Istituto Superiore di Sanità (Italian National Institute of Health)

CALL FOR PAPERS AND POSTERS
– deadline September 10, 2006

Conference objectives

- make researchers aware of the benefits of OA paradigm
- foster the implementation of on open access policies
- show the effects of the new publication model on research evaluation and impact
- promote cooperation between research institutions in Italy and abroad to share resources and experiences on institutional repositories

Target audience

Authors of publications in biomedicine, information specialists, managers of publication offices within research institutions.

- Interest areas for abstract presentation
- OA experiences of publication by researchers
- OA experiences in international editorial committees
- Proposals of services and policies promoting OA
- New evaluation possibilities offered by OA scientific publication

Scientific Committee

Claudio Di Benedetto (Data Management, Documentation, Library and Publishing Activities, ISS); Paola De Castro (Publishing Unit, ISS), Martino Grandolfo (Physics Dept, ISS),

Figure 11.1 Example of a first announcement of
a conference (*Cont'd*)

Paola Gargiulo (CASPUR, Rome), Valentina Comba (University of Bologna), Elisabetta Poltronieri (Publishing Unit, ISS)

Instructions for Abstract presentation

Abstracts shall include a descriptive and concise title, authors' names and surnames and affiliations, and a text of max 400 words in English. Abstracts shall be filled according to the format available at the conference website at http://www.iss.it

IMPORTANT DATES

September 10, 2006   Deadline for abstract presentation
October 10, 2006   Communication of accepted papers/
                      posters
December 10, 2006   Submission of full-text

For information, please contact: paola.decastro@iss.it   or elisabetta.poltronieri@iss.it

accepted for publication in professional journals, but in this cases, it is important to consider that publication times may be long, so it would be necessary to have the assurance that they will be printed in useful time before the deadline for abstract presentation.

Defining a conference programme

After the deadline for presenting abstracts is over, the scientific committee meets (or virtually meets) to select the most appropriate papers to be included in the *conference programme*. It is not always a simple task as sometimes there are too many relevant papers to be given space for oral presentations, and the choice may be difficult in order to prevent leaving out important research; however, the selection is a very difficult task and requires much care and sensitivity. *Selection criteria* should be carefully discussed and approved by committee members before making any decision and each contribution should be evaluated according to such criteria.

The basic selection criteria regards *quality assurance*; it will guide the decisions of the committee members (Is the research/activity/experience described of general interest? Is it original? is the methodology sound? Is the topic relevant for the conference objectives?, etc.). Some papers may not pass this first selection. However, even so, it may happen that it is not possible to accept all quality papers and it should be necessary a further shortlist. A second step in the selection may regard the necessity to maintain a balance among contributions coming from different countries—in case of international meetings—or different regions or institutions within the same country, etc.

In some cases, when there are many valuable contributions, the organizers may also decide to include one or more parallel sessions on specific topics, in order to allow more papers to be orally presented and discussed. This solution, however, may oblige the conference attendees to make a difficult choice among different parallel sessions in which they may be equally interested; sometimes delegates jump from one parallel session to the other in a useless attempt not to lose important information. When a parallel session is planned, the conference organizers should envisage a space in the programme for reporting on the activities and results achieved during the parallel sessions. The chairperson of the parallel session may be the best rapporteur to sum up the results of the parallel session, during a plenary session where all participants can attend.

The introduction of a *poster session* may represent another possible solution—together or in alternative with parallel sessions—when the number of valuable abstracts is too high with regards to the time allowed for presenting papers.

In this case, provided that there is enough space and the appropriate facilities in the conference area to place a certain number of posters, authors will be asked to produce a poster containing the main objectives and results of their research. Detailed instructions to authors of posters should be provided (poster size, font size, logistics, etc.), see chapter 13.

Posters should be located close to the conference hall (or in the conference hall itself) and will give authors the opportunity to informally discuss their work with other colleagues that are interested in their activities. Posters may also be more formally presented during a plenary session which allows brief comments on the activities therein described. The inclusion of a poster session may be envisaged already in the *call for papers* and authors may be asked to choose whether they wish to submit their paper for oral presentation or poster.

When defining the *time schedule* of a conference programme, it is advisable to give more time to invited speakers (generally 20–30 minutes), and less time to the other speakers (but no less than 10 minutes). Consider also that the chairperson should have the opportunity to properly introduce each speaker, add a short comment after their talks, and/or allow some question time soon after each speech, or at the end of the session. *Discussions* should be always welcome to permit the audience to take more actively part in the conference debate, add information, show interest, give feedback to the speakers, generate useful exchange of ideas and possibly develop new forms of collaborations.

Sometimes a conference may represent a good opportunity to organize *pre- or post-conference activities* that are closely connected with conference topics. It is the case of *training or education courses* that the same speakers or other experts taking part in the conference may deliver. This has the double advantage that teachers and students are already there and do not have to move to another place to attend a course, thus cutting down travel or accommodation expenses. Courses organized within a conference, however, should not be too long; it is advisable that their duration does not exceed one day, or half a day, otherwise they would require participants a commitment difficult to manage in terms of time, expenses and absence from work.

Once the Conference programme is defined, authors should be informed about their accepted or rejected works and receive detailed instructions on how to present their communications or posters, time allowed to speak, and facilities available.

Usually also a brief biographical note is required to better introduce them.

If the publication of proceedings is envisaged authors may be requested to sent their texts within a given date and according to specific instructions (see Chapter 6).

Sometimes an award may be envisaged for the best presentation or poster as a further incentive for a better quality.

A link containing very useful 'Picks from the literature on conferences' is available from the European Association of Health Information and Libraries (EAHIL) site at http://www .eahil.net/conferences_picks.htm

12

How to produce effective presentations

There are many opportunities for a librarian to talk to a small or large audience and use handouts or PowerPoint presentations with the objective of making communication more effective and easier to be remembered. Good presentations may be very useful in training activities or during conferences, workshops and meetings at different levels: they help speakers to follow the correct track and not to forget important ideas and, at the same time, focus on the most important concepts. Furthermore, visual images reinforce learning, help to better remember concepts and may transform a dull show into an exiting and durable exchange of information. Presentations may be useful also in e-learning projects. Yet, presentations alone can never replace a good speech or be a substitute for a full written text; in fact, they can even be misleading and completely lose their intended effect if they are not supported by an appropriate oral comment.

Presentations were initially used as a substitute for old slides or transparencies; then, as from the 1980s, PowerPoint has become a *de facto* standard providing speakers the greatest opportunities to show off. In fact, slides were widely used in the scientific world even before the use of PCs; however, technical support was required to produce them and last minute corrections were not possible.)

Yet, PowerPoint presentations can create a risk of making very poor figures if something does not work as expected, and add stress to the most controlled speaker.

As regards the more technical aspects of preparing a presentation, you can easily find in Internet demos in different languages explaining how to create and share dynamic and high-impact documents using PowerPoint or similar programs. We will not linger here on these details, but should reflect on the more general principles that guide a successful presentation. Even if the draw of powerful software may be very appealing, we should never exaggerate using elaborate effects that may create confusion and distract the audience, thus preventing them to focus on the relevant concepts. When preparing a presentation, never forget that you are trying to explain your ideas to other people and it is not for yourself to show how smart, intelligent, cultured and technological you are!

Whenever you decide to include an image or text taken from another publication (including those available in Internet) be sure to include full details of the source and do not infringe any copyright law. For teaching purposes, there are generally no restrictions on the use of images (provided that the source is duly cited), but the same does not apply when presentations are distributed online or printed. Permission should always be received for that.

Before getting to work

Presentations can capture audience interest and keep it there, even when you are dealing with difficult concepts. The attention curve inevitably decreases after the first 10 minutes and a good presentation can help in keeping that interest. Before getting to work on a presentation, bear in mind that people cannot listen or focus on important concepts and, at the same time, read a long text on a screen and appreciate its graphics. Therefore, it is advisable that you reflect on the following points.

Consider your audience and time available

Before deciding on text or graphics, carefully consider the characteristics of the audience you are reaching. Are they young or adults, or both? Are you addressing a local, national or international group? Think of their expectancies, their interests, what they need or wish to know and what they already know about your topic.

At the same time reflect on the time at your disposal; it is useless to prepare a long presentation if you will not have time to display it properly. Generally, one slide takes 1 minute, but there may be difficult concepts expressed in one slide that need more time to be clarified and others (images or quotations, for example) that just need a few seconds. Remember that too many slides lose their effect if your presentation is hurried. When time is very short or when the audience is made up of just very few people, a presentation may even be useless, and it may be better to use handout material or simple flipcharts.

Organize your ideas

Organizing ideas and developing them into a logical structure is fundamental for any successful presentation. You may start by writing down your first thoughts as large themes, discuss them with your colleagues for immediate feedback, and carefully think and define which is the best way to present your topics. Find an original way to show basic concepts before developing them into a given number of slides (the term slide here is inappropriately commonly used to indicate a screen).

Choose a graphical design

All slides should have a uniform layout, including text and graphics: each element contributes to communicate something, call attention and create emotions. Fonts (type, size and style) have their own language, as well as colours and all the other graphical elements appearing in each slide, including background images. All elements must be carefully selected to create a well balanced and pleasant presentation; this may require much time and many tests before reaching a satisfactory result.

Check if there are any 'Instructions to authors' and appropriate facilities for presentation

Never take for granted that the appropriate facilities for presentations are always available in any location you are going to speak.

Before getting to work on a presentation, you should know how much time your presentation can take, and be assured that you will have the appropriate facilities to use for it to work. Most conference halls are now well equipped with projectors and computers; conference organizers generally provide instructions to authors including information on presentations. Yet, there may be occasions (smaller meetings or distant places) where facilities for presentations do not exist or do not work as you would have expected (always ask which version of the software has been installed so you can be prepared!). Sometimes you may be required to take your own laptop. Don't forget the appropriate plugs and converters and take a pen drive or a CD with your presentation, including fonts (if not standard), music or movie files that you used in the presentation.

Suggested structure and scheme

Once you have considered all preliminaries, you can concentrate on the structure and scheme of your presentation and start working on the production of slides. One of the main advantages of a presentation is that once you have learned some basic commands it is easy to: modify the entire structure, change, add, delete or postpone slides, modify texts, images, background, fonts, etc. It will not be difficult to create a model to be applicable to every slide, or select one of the many free models available online; the risk is that you will not be original, but it will surely work!

You should practise your presentation until you reach a satisfactory result. Concepts that are difficult to explain orally can be quickly and easily grasped thanks to visual aids. Presentation and a good talk should be able to transmit some kind of emotion, which is basic to create a positive attitude to learn, perceive, reflect on any theme. You should have a good grasp of the subject you are presenting, be prepared in advance, consider timing, check technical facilities and rehearse many times to feel sure that everything will work.

A good structure for presentation consists of the following recommended elements.

- *Introduction.* The first slide should include the title of your presentation, your name and affiliation, e-mail if you wish, and possibly the place and date of the event.

- *Main themes.* An initial slide, including an outline of the *main themes* you will cover, is highly recommended to make the audience aware of what they are going to listen and prepare them to focus on the most important points. It is comparable with the table of contents of a book.

- *Body of the presentation.* It includes a well organized sequence of slides that may be grouped under separate sections, if appropriate, like the chapters in a book. Always keep in mind that each section must be well balanced with the others and proportionate with the given time schedule. Text should be kept to a minimum; in presentations concepts replace sentences—that is why linguistic barriers can be easily overcome! Graphs (bars, pies, lines) are better than tables that include much data that cannot be easily read at a distance. If you need to point out numbers, include only a minimum set of data on the screen. Images that are not clearly reproduced only add confusion and distraction.

- *Conclusions*. A closing slide or group of slides containing the summary of the main discussion points is highly recommended to determine ideas. It must be brief and simple to reinforce the aims of the presentation and leave a positive feeling they have been accomplished.

It is always advisable to leave time for questions. Discussions show interest and although speakers may be apprehensive about them, these are evidence that the presentation has raised curiosity and created awareness. If you feel unprepared to answer some questions, say so clearly, and postpone the answer for another time when you will be able to give the required explanation.

With regard to the technical scheme suggested for a professional presentation, bear in mind that there are some common elements in any slide including:

- *Background*, that is design and colours on the back of each slide; only the first slide may be different from the others, but they all should follow the same graphical theme. Select a clear background that will not distract the audience and permit easy reading of the text. Check colours and anticipate that conditions in the hall may not always be as you would expect in terms of light, quality and size of display, etc.

- *Graphical elements* may appear on one or other parts of the slide (corners, upper, lower, middle part) to make it more pleasant, but they must not distract the audience and must produce a well balanced effect. Colours should be carefully selected and kept to a minimum. A single background colour, or colour family, throughout the presentation guarantees continuity. You can separate broad sections (chapters) inside the body of the presentation by changing background colours, but always keep changes to a minimum, unless your purpose is to shock or create fun!

- *Font or set of fonts* to be used for the different hierarchical levels of the text. The use of many types of fonts is confusing. To stress changes you may use bold, italic, capital letters, underline, quotations and/or colour to emphasize key points or words. Standard fonts are recommended to make sure that you will find them on all PCs available in the conference hall, otherwise you should be able to install the proper font before presentation, but this may add more stress.

- *Progressive numbering* of slides helps keeping track of the sequence, as in a book; sometimes it may be useful to include the total number to of slides preceded by the number of the slide (e.g. 6/60) to let the audience know the progress of the presentation.

- *Title, place and date of the event* may be added as a footnote; it will be very useful when you use or reuse the presentation or make it available online for different purposes.

Finally, remember to state your facts in a simple, concise and interesting manner. Tell a story that is appealing, add your personal experience and try to evaluate efficacy in advance.

The best speakers are not always the people who know more about a topic, but those who are able to select information to better convey a message, those who are able to communicate and involve their audience and not just inform them about facts and data that will be easily forgot, and last but not least, those who have time to be prepared and rehearse repeatedly.

13

How to produce effective posters

Posters generally represent a good opportunity to take part in a conference where there are many communications trying to get the attention of the scientific committee (after a 'call for papers', see Chapter 11), but not all can be accepted for oral presentations. Poster abstracts may be included in the Conference abstract book and also the Proceedings may accept extended papers related to posters.

A poster is a means of showing an activity or project, share ideas, create collaborations, and receive feedback. Some conferences programmes include a poster session where posters' authors can orally explain their work and receive comments. A successful poster may be developed into an article, a booklet, or other documents for wider distribution.

Librarians may wish to produce a poster independently from a conference presentation to inform about an important activity or service with the objective of making users aware of the new opportunities offered by their library.

As regards the use of textual and graphic material, techniques followed for the realization of a poster have many tracts in common with the production of PowerPoint presentations (Chapter 12), but unlike presentations, posters are static products that should catch attention, be understood and remembered also without oral comments by the authors.

Unlike journal articles or books, posters may not undergo a strict revision process before appearing, apart from the fact that abstracts associated with the proposal of a conference poster should be accepted by a conference scientific committee and that approval may be required by your institution for any document you produce, according to more or less formal procedures.

Before getting to work

Why make a poster

Before starting work you should clarify the main objectives of your poster; consider the intended audience, the place where it should be exhibited, and focus on the title and authorship.

Remember that a poster is not an article of reduced font size that you can just stuck on a board, nor is it a presentation with a limited number of slides. A poster needs a proper design, a sound structure and professional skills to be properly realized.

Furthermore, posters cannot be corrected at the last minute as presentations are, so if there is a mistake in the final print or if images are not as clear as they appeared on the screen, either you have it printed again (and that may cause additional stress and expense), or there is practically nothing to do except to correct it manually—but in most cases the result is that errors will be highlighted rather then hidden!

Poster production should not be underestimated; it may require much time until you are satisfied with your product, as in all creative work. The graphical design plays a very important part in the transmission of the message in a visual form, and a poor graphic may dramatically reduce the impact of your poster or even induce not to read it at all.

Are you aware of dimensions and spaces?

Before starting the project you should know how much space you have; so check if there are instructions available on the conference website, or ask them to the conference organizers to avoid any disappointment at the moment of fixing your poster. Sometimes they may be too large for the given space thus becoming useless, other times they may be too small and the effect is equally upsetting.

How will you print the poster?

Good printing often makes a difference, but it depends on the equipment available in your institution, or on the budget at your disposal to pay for a service. If you can have a poster printed by a quality plotter and you can select a good quality paper for it, unexpectedly, you may produce good results. However, if you do not have a plotter or your budget does not allow printing the poster outside your institution, you might be obliged to use standard sheets of paper and mount the poster yourself with unexpected bad results! It is important to know all this before starting the project to find possible remedies in advance.

Balancing content, structure and graphics

Content: make a sketch of your ideas, select the main topics and arrange the order

The first step in building up a poster is to make a draft and clarify your ideas: see if your conceptual scheme can work, in particular include all the essential parts of your project, cut out all irrelevant details, and decide on possible headings, graphs and pictures, if any. The layout and graphic design will come later and may be influenced by the content that you wish to show.

The presentation of the intellectual content should follow a logical structure that will allow readers to immediately identify its object and aims without reading all the details.

The main title and all the subheadings are very important and should capture attention and be read at a distance. There is not one structure that fits all topics, but a logical order is essential in the presentation of any fact.

If you are dealing with research work for a conference poster it may be convenient to organize the text according to the following scheme.

- Poster title

- Authors' names and institutional affiliation (logo if appropriate)

- Introduction (including background information and aims of the study)

- Materials and methods (objects of the study and stages of its development)

- Results and discussion (main results achieved or expected and discussions points)

- Title, place and date of the conference where the poster is presented.

The titles of each subheading may contain important messages replacing the more formal headings (such as introduction, material and methods, results), to stress the main points of your work and make them immediately evident to the readers.

Useless words should be cut down, and sentence length and complexity should be reduced to a minimum thus avoiding unnecessary detail: people standing in front of a poster will highly appreciate simple wording and short sentences are easy to remember.

Layout: how to define spaces for text and graphics

As regards the layout you should define a 'Visual grammar' that is a graphic hierarchy allowing readers to identify the most important parts of your poster.

Within the dimensions assigned by the organizers (usually 70 × 100 cm) you should arrange your text and graphics, taking into consideration that the main titles are to be read at a distance and that blank space helps readers to fix on the other important elements of the page. Too much text does not work, as well as the inclusion of too many graphical elements creating visual chaos and preventing effective communication of good content that is always the pre-requisite of any quality work.

The space within the page may be divided into columns or boxes that allow quick reading and some clues (arrows, bullets, numbers or other graphical signs) may be added to facilitate understanding of each part.

Posters can be created using software packages, such as PowerPoint, used for presentation, allowing to print in the appropriate size.

A few final tips on text, illustrations and colour will help you to produce a good poster.

- *Text.* Always avoid long lines that are difficult to read, and keep font size at least 24 points in text and no less than 36 for headings.

- *Illustrations* (graphs, photos and tables). They play a very important role in a poster, often prevailing on text and allowing fast communication of difficult concepts or relations. They must be clear, simple and of good quality. Remember that any image will be enlarged when printed in a poster, so possible faults or imperfections will clearly show. Line graphs, bars, pie charts are always better than tables, but if you have to include a table to stress numbers, make it simple and limit figures to the essential.

- *Colour.* It is very important to capture attention and emphasize concepts. You should be able to create contrast, but do not go over the top by using too many colours or families of colours.

As for any other written documents, it is advisable to get colleagues' comment on a draft before printing, and receive useful feedback that will help improve your work.

14

Addressing the media

Speaking as well as writing for the media can create major involvement of both the general public and opinion leaders to attract attention and increase awareness on specific issues related to library services or collections, or special events associated with or organized by a library or inside it.

Media involvement contributes to create change, develop a public image of libraries and the role of librarians, as well as attracting new resources and users. Of course, all messages spread through the media require an appropriate strategy that is directly dependent from the library mission, the socio-cultural context in which it operates and the final objective of the communication.

The American Library Association released a very useful Communication Handbook for Libraries in 2007. This handbook was designed to help librarians develop and maintain effective relations with the media and obtain support for their programmes, with minimal use of resources. You can download the handbook from the ALA website: http://www.ala.org/ala/pio/mediarelationsa/availablepiomat/ commhandbook.htm/.

In general, media can be reached through the following channels:

- *Print* (newspaper, magazines, journals, etc.) through news, announcements, editorials, letters, viewpoints, comments on events, publications or images related to or produced by libraries, etc.

- *Internet* through, news, blogs, chats, discussion or mailing lists, etc.
- *Radio and television networks* through news, announcements, interviews, talks, commentaries, etc.

If you work in the library of an institution that has its own press office, always apply to them before talking to or writing for any media: they will know how to manage events and give you the appropriate advice for every circumstance. Personal contacts, in fact, are extremely important in organizing the information flow with the media. For this reason, press offices have *ad hoc* and updated media lists, including names of useful contacts, their specialties, working hours, office and cell phones, addresses, the journals, radio or TV networks for which they work, etc. In this way, a press office is able to select only reliable people to address to without interferences, where necessary. Librarians may prepare fact sheets and background information in advance to be distributed among journalists to support any news at the right moment.

In absence of a press office within your institution, before accepting any commitment, it is important to be informed about the journalist's perspectives, the journal aims, the type of interview (taped or live) and its use (who else is involved); then decide if it is convenient for you to accept an interview and who may be the best person to do that. Spokespersons should be aware of the right way to create a story for the media, have time to prepare it, and clearly express ideas and facts in a way that people can easily understand, without using jargon. They should also be able to manage possible crises or difficult questions.

When talking to journalists, time is always very short, so news must be given in the most effective and concise way to clearly highlight your message and its objective.

The same clarity and directness is required when you wish to write for the media. You should be able to deliver your news in a concise and attractive way by applying the rule of the five Ws:

1. *who* (people involved in the event)

2. *what* (description of the event)

3. *when* (exact date and hour of the event)

4. *where* (place of event)

5. *why* (explain the relevance of the event).

The media advisory and a news release are among the most common tools to spread information through selected media lists.

Media advisory

A *media advisory* is generally printed on the letterhead of your institution, including its logo to assure the required official format. It contains concise and essential information on upcoming events given in a standard format including:

- the term *media advisory* (generally at top left corner of the page),
- the date of the event and contact person,
- a headline containing the most important information,
- the answers to the five Ws as indicated above,
- a brief description of your institution/library, at the bottom,
- as a closing, type # # # to indicate the end of the advisory.

News release

A *news release* is more complex than the media advisory. It also contains quotes and facts to create a story that journalists can directly use or reuse to create their own story. Information is presented according to the inverted pyramid method: the most important facts are first to catch attention and then details are given. The standard format for a news release includes:

- the term *news release* (generally at top left corner of the page) and its number,
- the words *for immediate release* and date of the event and contact person,
- a headline (one line) and subhead containing the most important information and the name of your institution,
- the first paragraph capturing attention,
- other paragraphs, including answers to the five W's and quotes from spokespersons, giving their names and qualifications,
- a brief description of your institution/library, at the bottom,
- as a closing, type # # # to indicate the end of the advisory.

A news release may exceed one page in length; if so, be sure to add the convention '–more–', at the end of the first page and print again the title of the release at the top of the second page, writing 'page 2'. A news release may be included in a press folder containing also other relevant documents that may be very useful to reporters.

Final considerations

The best final advice to conclude this volume is to be always clear and honest in any form of communication, either oral or written: explain your facts in a logical and easy way and concentrate on the needs and expectations of your audience: library users, peers, supervisors, editors, etc. Reflect on the important elements of the communication process: the message you wish to get across, your target, and the best way to realize it, also considering the very important role that any interfering noise may play.

Sometimes communication is not effective just because it is not clear; also in *vis á vis* communication, the person you are talking to may not be ready to listen or may not have the appropriate tools, attitude or will to understand what you are saying.

It is always important to be honest and firm in sustaining your ideas with your colleagues, supervisors, referees, but at the same time be able to listen to their suggestions and ready to revise your work, if necessary.

For any type of professional communication, the planning stage is fundamental; it may require much unexpected time and effort, but it helps save much possible inconvenience as well as much time and money. Carefully decide on authors and collaborations whether you choose written document production (be it a journal article, book, or even leaflet or technical report) or oral communication (e.g. conference, workshops, interviews, etc.). Therefore, you can assign responsibility and give credit to the work without ambiguity. It is also important to obtain the required permission from supervisors, especially in formal or official communications.

Under any circumstances it is fundamental not to neglect ethical principles, technical rules and traditions governing professional communication in each field. On the other hand, it is also advisable to cautiously evaluate any possible alternative in document production at all stages; do not say your work is over until you are really satisfied with it and feel you that you can sustain it in front of the most challenging audience.

Furthermore, as everything changes very fast, be sure to be always updated and never take for granted rules and procedures (instructions to authors, internal procedures, required approvals, etc.) that worked perfectly until yesterday because they may have changed just today!

As a final remark, in this highly technological society, it is important not to become too dependent on technology that inevitably invests all aspects of our professional activities and our private lives as well. We are very grateful to technology that helps us produce and disseminate quality information with reduced time and effort, yet, it is always very important and wise to first focus on the content you wish to transmit and then use technology to help achieve your aims.

Recommended reading

There is a large amount of international and national literature on how to communicate, how to produce documents, how to talk in public or produce a powerful presentations; there are also many international and national standards, guidelines and recommendations on specific editorial issues and computer software providing useful guides; journals issue instructions to authors that are often very detailed, conference organizers issue practical guidelines as well, and professional associations produce guidelines on specific sources. Many of these sources are freely available on the Internet.

If you do not have much time, we suggest referring to the following three guidelines as a useful starting point for further reading on how to publish a journal article, how to produce a technical report, and how to maintain effective relations with the media.

The *Uniform requirements for manuscripts submitted to biomedical journals*, available from: http://www.icmje.org/, regularly updated, and also translated into different languages. They are produced by the International Committee of Medical Journal Editors (ICMJE) and now adopted by the most important biomedical journals. They are better known as *Vancouver style* as they were first released in Vancouver (British Columbia) in 1978 where a small group of editors of general medical journals met to establish guidelines for the format of manuscripts submitted to their journals. Since then the guidelines are regularly updated, which is why they can now be considered as a basic reference tool for all those who wish to publish an article—indeed not only in the biomedical field—and quickly learn the fundamental rules for a correct presentation of a journal article. The first editions of these guidelines were basically concerned with the formats of manuscripts and in particular bibliographic references. Now 'Vancouver style' mostly includes ethical principles related to the publication and links to the site of the National Library of Medicine for instructions on how to write a correct bibliographic reference.

The *Guidelines for the production of scientific and technical reports: how to write and distribute grey literature*, available from: http://www.glisc.info. They are produced by the Grey Literature International Steering committee in 2006, and are informally known as 'Nancy Style' as they were first conceived during the 7th International Conference on Grey Literature held in Nancy, France in 2005. These Guidelines, regularly updated and now available in English, Italian, French, German and Spanish, were created primarily to help authors and producers of grey literature in their mutual task of creating and distributing accurate, clear, easily accessible reports and similar documents, in the respect of the basic editorial principles. They may be very useful for librarians who are not supported by editorial experts to publish their documents, as it happens for documents of grey literature. As 'Vancouver style', also 'Nancy Style' includes ethical principles related to the process of writing, evaluating, revising and making available documents that are informally produced.

A Communication Handbook for Libraries, the handbook produced by American Library Association, available from http://www.ala.org/ala/pio/mediarelationsa/availablepiomat/commhandbook.htm/.

It is conceived for libraries and provides easy tips to develop and maintain effective relations with the media with minimal use of resources. Starting with the basics, it explains what publicity is and how it can help a library attract attention, create interest and gain support. It is rich in very practical examples and fits the most diverse situations.

Here follows a selection of further useful readings that inspired this book.

References are mainly to English texts, although there is also much on offer that is useful material for non-English speaking readers.

Useful reading

Albert T. *The A–Z of medical writing*. London: BMJ Publishing Books; 2000.

De Castro P, Guida S, Sagone MB (Eds). *Diciamolo chiaramente*. Rome: Il Pensiero Scientifico; 2004.

European Association of Science Editors. *Science editors' handbook*. Old Woking (UK): EASE; 2007.

Freeman JV, Walters FJ, Campbell MJ. *How to display data*. Oxford: BMJ Books/Blackwell Publishing; 2008.

Gustavii B. *How to write and illustrate a scientific paper*. Lund: Studentlitteratur; 2000.

Hall GM (Ed.). *How to present at meetings*. 2nd edn. BMJ Books. Oxford: Blackwell Publishing; 2007.

Hames I. *Peer review and manuscript management in scientific journals. Guidelines for good practice*. Oxford: Blackwell Publishing, in association with the Association of Learned and Professional Society Publishers (ALPSP); 2007.

Huth EJ. *How to write and publish papers in the medical sciences*. 2nd edn. Baltimore, MD: Williams & Wilkins; 1990.

Jacobs N (Ed.) *Open access: key strategic, technical and economic aspects*. Oxford: Chandos Publishing; 2006.

Matthews JR, Bowen JM, Matthews RW. *Successful scientific writing. A step-by-step guide for biological and medical sciences.* Cambridge: Cambridge University Press; 2000.

Nadziejka DE. *Levels of technical editing.* Council of Science Editors Guidelines No. 4. Reston, VA: Council of Biology Editors; 1999.

Oghojafor K. *E-book publishing success. How anyone can write, compile and sell e-books on the Internet.* Oxford: Chandos Publishing; 2005.

Patrias K. *Citing medicine: the NLM guide for authors, editors, and publishers.* 2nd edn. Bethesda, MD: National Library of Medicine (US); 2007. Available from http://www .nlm.nih.gov/citingmedicine/.

Peat J, Elliot E, Baur L, Keena V. *Scientific writing. Easy when you know how.* London: BMJ Publishing Group; 2002.

Seely J. *Oxford guide to effective writing and speaking.* New York: Oxford University Press; 2005.

Style Manual Committee-Council of Biology Editors. *Scientific style and format: the CBE manual for authors, editors, and publishers.* 6th edn. New York: Cambridge University Press; 1994.

Wager E. *Getting research published. An A to Z of publication strategy.* Oxford: Radcliffe Publishing. 2005.

World Association of Medical Editors. *WAME syllabus for prospective and newly appointed editors.* Available from: http://www.wame.org/resources/editor-s-syllabus/.

Index

2778 63

Printed in the United States
218834BV00002B/6/P

9 781843 343783